had a glass

TOP 100 WINES FOR 2009
UNDER $20

Kenji Hodgson | James Nevison

whitecap

Whitecap Books is known for its expertise in the cookbook market, and has produced some of the
most innovative and familiar titles found in kitchens across North America. Visit our website at
www.whitecap.ca.

Edited by Melva McLean
Proofread by Joan E. Templeton
Cover design by Five Seventeen, Setareh Ashrafologhalai, and Michelle Mayne
Food icons and occasion icon by Five Seventeen
Interior design and illustrations by Jacqui Thomas
Typeset by Setareh Ashrafologhalai
Photography by Jan Westendorp, James Nevison, and Kenji Hodgson
Photo editing by Jan Westendorp

Printed in Canada by Friesens

LIBRARY AND ARCHIVES CANADA CATALOGUING IN PUBLICATION

Hodgson, Kenji
    Had a glass : top 100 wines for 2009 under $20 / Kenji Hodgson, James Nevison.

Includes index.
ISBN 978-1-55285-937-7

    1. Wine and wine making—Canada. I. Nevison, James II. Title.

TP548.H628 2008   641.2'20971   C2008-902143-6

The publisher acknowledges the financial support of the Government of Canada through the Book
Publishing Industry Development Program (BPIDP) and the Province of British Columbia through the
Book Publishing Tax Credit.

08 09 10 11 12 5 4 3 2 1

contents

preface—the juice

Great wine is hard to find. Four editions into *Had a Glass*, we can report that wine is still a moving target (or at least a fluid one). True, it gets somewhat easier if you know what you're looking for, the educated guesses more likely to hit the mark. But picking amazing wine is always going to be an uphill quest. After all, we're talking about an agricultural product subject to all the vagaries Mother Nature throws grapes' way. That's the fun of it (or at least it should be). If the challenge didn't exist, we'd all just crack a Bud.

But let's forget about great wine for a second. What is *good* wine? While the pat answer is "any wine that you like," we say kick that cliché and start answering this tough question seriously. A good wine is one that represents. That is, first and foremost, wine is about diversity, and a good wine should show it. Why else would it be shipped around the world? If our olfactory curiosities could be satiated by wine made from within a hundred mile radius, then there wouldn't be acres of shelving devoted to the beverage. Instead, we can cruise into any decent wine shop or liquor store and see a gallery of vinous potables. The best will assert their personalities. We might not get along with all of them, but good wine speaks its mind.

Secondly, wine is about flavour. We can geek out on this appellation or that variety all we like (or until our wives tell us to cut the wine chatter), but at the end of the day, we drink the stuff. And it had better taste good.

Had a Glass points to good wine. We hope that readers, after they taste a few wines, will consider a number of them great, but from good to great is a personal, subjective call that we hope you have fun exploring. For this 2009 edition we have combed every shelf to bring you the goods—the unique, the exciting, and the delicious—all the while making sure you can afford to sip seven days a week.

The Old Is New

2009 is all about balance. The more people we talk to—and share a glass with—the more we hear the call for wines that aren't going to do a coup d'état at the dinner table. It's less about the fruit bomb and more about the finesse. It's about wine that goes with food. Even more so, it's about wines that deliver the complete package. Whether they're white or red, light- or full-bodied, oaked or unoaked, we're after wines with harmony.

The pendulum has swung. In *Had a Glass 2009* there are more old-school wines than ever before. Italy has come out swinging like the Great Bambino. France is as strong a contender as ever. Spain is stomping the grapes. And even Germany and Austria are delivering the gems at great prices. Big selection, big value, and big up! What's that about the strength of the Euro?

Red Goes White

Speaking of pendulums, continuing the trend from last year we are officially off the red. Well not entirely—when it comes to steaks on the barbie, the Sauvignon Blanc isn't yet replacing the Shiraz—but more than ever, white wines are what's in our glasses. Not that the two hues can't coexist, and our cellar would never be complete without some sublime rosés, but whether you chalk it up to taste trends, food friendliness, or just plain colour coordination, in 2009 the wines sans skins keep showing off.

Wood Takes a Split

Say goodbye to woody wines as wine furniture takes a back seat. The amount of oak applied to wine has hit a saturation point, as our palates have seen enough vanilla, smoke, toast, and caramel. A little lumber is fine, but we believe in balance. Let the character of the wine show, without the smokescreen.

Tasting through hundreds of wines this year, we found a cord that tasted like a sawmill; thankfully we found many more that exuded a dexterous symmetry of flavour. It's the latter that made the cut.

Getting On with It
Our palates well fatigued, we think we have zeroed in on a lip-smacking list of a hundred wines for all to enjoy. From the beginning wine drinker to the cellarable wine geek, the vinously curious to the ABC-diehard looking for another Cabernet, there's a wine for everyone in *Had a Glass 2009*.

Sip on,

Kenji & James

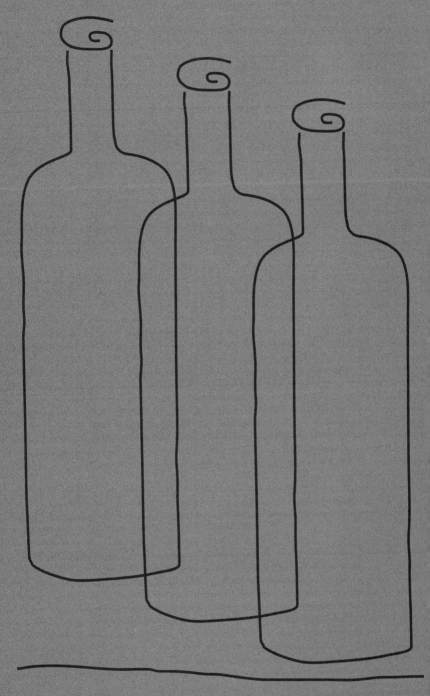

a brief guide to
wine enjoyment

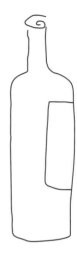

Had a Glass?

Had a Glass gives you the wine goods. In a veritable sea of vinous choice, *Had a Glass* points you in the right direction and makes sure you surface with a good bottle. And it won't cost you big money. The 100 wines in this book check in at under $20.

Each wine is here for a reason, whether it's perfect with a steak, for a picnic, or simply as a stand-alone sipper. And each one is a wine that we like to buy and drink.

The wines come from a swath of countries and are made from a mix of grape varieties. They're reds and whites, sweets and dries. It's wine diversity that we think you'll enjoy.

Pick a page, read the blurb, get the wine, and see what you think. Repeat often.

But remember: Quaffing the grape juice is tons of fun as long as you wine in moderation. Know your limit and always have a designated driver. Such is the path to true wine appreciation.

Buyer Beware

In compiling this list, we've taken care to select wines that are widely available. We all deserve good wine, no matter where we are.

Every effort has been made to ensure prices and vintages were correct at the time of publication. That said, the vagaries of wine buying and copy deadlines conspire against us. The good buys sell out, and the hot wines are subject to price increases (including fuel surcharges, of course).

Use this book as a starting point for your wine-buying adventures. Great bottles are out there, and like all good hunts, the fun is in the search.

The Value Proposition

"Value" is a dirty word, and its utterance leads to trouble. Like scoring wine on a hundred-point scale, its objective scaffolding tries to prop up a subjective framework. "Value" is at best squishy and hard to pin down. But whether you're after price rollbacks at Wal-Mart or one-of-a-kind designer pieces, true value occurs when returns exceed expectations.

Here's how value is applied in *Had a Glass*
Our bank accounts set the upper limit of our wine budget at $20. Sure, on occasion we may spend more, but overall we toe the $20 line. From our research, we know most of you feel the same. We all love getting a great $15 bottle of wine. But we love cracking into a tasty $10 bottle even more.

Had a Glass celebrates those wines that give you the best bottle for the buck: the $10 wines that seem like $15, the $15 bottles that stand out, the $20 wines that taste like more. We see wine as an everyday beverage, not as a luxury—an enjoyable accessory to good living.

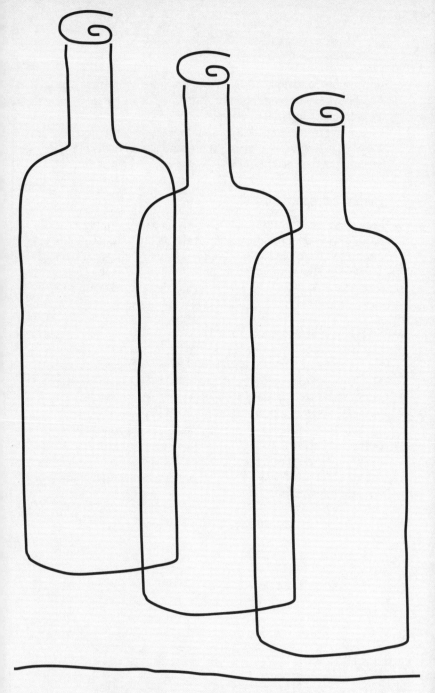

how to taste wine

Drinking wine and tasting wine are two different pastimes. If your only desire is to drink, by all means turn the page and get on to the reviews.

But, if you're ready to take your wine relationship to the next level, it's time to commit to proper tasting technique. It will add to your wine enjoyment as well as permit a complete sensory evaluation of the wine in your glass using taste, sight, smell, and feel.

We're tired of "A good wine is a wine you like." Sure, at the end of the day it's a subjective thing where your opinion matters, but what makes a wine good? After you understand how to taste wine you'll be equipped to make that call.

The Four Steps

Here's the wine-tasting process in four simple steps.

Step 1—The Look
Tilt the wineglass away from yourself and observe the colour against a white background. White wine can be pallid yellow to deep gold, and reds range from the rich crimson of velvet drapes to the neon of raspberry Kool-Aid. Young white wines may have the brilliant sheen of white gold while older reds often have complex tones of browns superimposed on sombre claret. Whites are typically clear, nearly transparent, whereas a red may be slightly cloudy with sediment.

Step 2—The Swirl
Swirl the wineglass—either on the table or in the air—to draw out the aromas of a wine. Let the wine paint the sides of the glass with long, smooth tears (or "legs"). Note that these indicate texture and viscosity, not necessarily quality.

Step 3—The Smell
Smelling is wine intimacy. A deep inhale will reveal what the wine is about. Don't be afraid to put your nose into the glass. A wine may have the aromas of fruit (melons, berries, cherries), of wood (vanilla or smoke), or of spice (pepper or cloves). You may also get a whiff of less likely aromas, such as earth, diesel, and leather. Surprising, maybe, but this is what makes wine exciting.

Step 4—The Taste
Take a generous sip of wine. Swirl it in your mouth. The consistency may be "thin" like skim milk (light-bodied) or more like 2% milk (full-bodied). Let your tongue taste the different elements of the wine: any sweetness from residual sugars, any tartness from acid, or any bitterness from alcohol. Tannins may dry your gums, making you pucker. Spitting is optional.

Taking Notes

Whether you carry a leather-bound wine journal or scribble on a paper napkin, take wine notes whenever you can. At the very least, jot the name of the wine and a thumbs-up or -down. This will save you from repeating the phrase, "I had a great wine last night . . . I think it had a picture of something on the label."

We use a tasting sheet like this:

TASTING NOTES

	WINE 1	WINE 2	WINE 3
TASTING DATE			
WINE NAME • Vintage • Region • Price			
COLOUR • Straw Gold • Claret Purple • Clarity			
SMELL • Fruity • Woody • Spicy • Floral • Earthy			
TASTE • Sweetness • Acidity • Bitterness			
FEEL • Body • Tannin • Finish			
CONCLUSION • Balance • Quality • Do I Like This Wine?			

Usual Aromas

We know that wine smells like wine, but what else does wine smell like? There are infinite aromas in fermented grape juice, and everyone smells something different, but here are a few usual aromas to get you started:

Red Wine	White Wine
• Blackberry	• Apple
• Raspberry	• Pear
• Plum	• Peach
• Vanilla	• Grapefruit
• Earthiness	• Honey

Unusual Aromas

And then there are the weird scents. This is where wine gets interesting. A healthy imagination when tasting wine is always good.

- Barnyard
- Leather chaps
- Wet fur
- Socks
- Ripe cheese

Flights of Fancy

Becoming a good wine taster is all about tasting wines. The more wines you try, the better your frame of reference. A great way to build your database and bolster your tasting skills is to approach wine in "flights." Create a flight by lining up a few wines that share a common theme. Tasting these side by side is like taking three pairs of jeans into the changing room.

Here are a few wine flights to get you started:

Flight 1—Homegrown Heroes

Everyone likes to back the home team, and it's all the more exciting when there's something to cheer about, which makes what's happening in the Okanagan Valley so great. For such a young wine region, British Columbia is putting out some increasingly tasty vino, and as grape growers and winemakers continue to hone their skills and knowledge of the Okanagan's unique terroir, things should only get better. Already we're seeing sub-regions take shape, with white grapes thriving in cooler climate zones of the north, to big reds being planted in the desert-hot south. Here's a flight from Kelowna to Osoyoos, with a stop in Okanagan Falls for good measure.

A. St. Hubertus Chasselas (page 60)

B. See Ya Later Ranch Gewürztraminer (page 62)

C. Nk'Mip Cellars Merlot (page 134)

Flight 2—A Noseful: Aromatic Whites
Aromatic whites are some of the most fun wines to taste. They're the types of wines that really jump out of the glass as you swirl, providing great instant gratification. They're also great wines for beginners to try; their strong, standout aromas scream to be noticed and can help tasters gain confidence identifying wine traits.

A. d'Arenberg Stump Jump White (page 56)

B. Boutari Moschofilero (page 69)

C. Valckenberg Gewürztraminer (page 64)

Flight 3—Groovy Grenache
Grenache—or *Garnacha* as it's known in Spain—is a groovy type of grape. Boisterous and fruity, it has typically been used as a blending partner (usually with Syrah) to flesh out a wine, but is increasingly shining on its own. Regardless, Grenache brings fun to the bottle. Its sun-worshipping, soft, and fruity style screams that it's here for a good time (not necessarily a long time).

A. Sorrento Grenache (page 116)

B. Louis Bernard Côtes du Rhône (65 percent Grenache/35 percent Syrah) (page 102)

C. Espelt Sauló (60 percent Garnacha/40 percent Cariñena) (page 100)

Self-Help for Wine Monotony

If your wining has been monotonous of late, try these wine-buying strategies and never be stuck on the same bottle again.

Branching out

When you find yourself smitten by a particular grape, expand on your infatuation by exploring similar bottles from around the wine world. As an example, take Cabernet Sauvignon. Still reigning as the "King of Grapes," this noble red, prized by collectors for its richness and cellarability, can certainly command royal prices. Thankfully, this year we've amassed a number of notable Cabs, which offer a great learning excursion.

Start in South America, where Cabernet Sauvignon thrives in the continent's sun-drenched vineyards. Terra Andina (page 86) in Chile offers a great example of bold, New World style. Next, head across the Atlantic Ocean to South Africa, where the De Wet family's Excelsior Estate (page 108) produces Cabs in the Breede River Valley. Finally, complete a true global dalliance with Cabernet and pick up a bottle of Galil (page 122) from Israel.

Love of the land

Certain parts of the world make certain types of wine. This is often denoted on the bottle by appellation, or where the wine originated. Flipping through the pages this year you'll see some great wine locales, such as "McLaren Vale" and "Toro." If you like the wine of a particular app, try others from the same locale.

A classic place to start is France's Côtes du Rhône, a storied A.O.C. (Appellation d'Origine Contrôlée). Both the Saint Cosme (page 135) and Paul Jaboulet (page 126) hail from this heartland of vinous France, where rich and sometimes spicy red blends are produced—and often imitated in other wine regions of the world. Both bottles are great examples of the diverse drinkability of the Rhône wines.

Trading up

A winery commonly makes different tiers of wines—the Toyota and the Lexus. *Had a Glass* is all about the Toyotas, but if you like what you're test-driving, look for the luxury version.

Local Okanagan producer Golden Mile Cellars crafts a number of fantastic wines from their Oliver winery. We find their white label Chardonnay (page 74), a particularly fine example of BC's potential with this noble white grape. That said, if you're looking to kick it up a notch and have a few extra dollars to spend, it's worth checking out Golden Mile's Black Arts tier, the winery's top offerings.

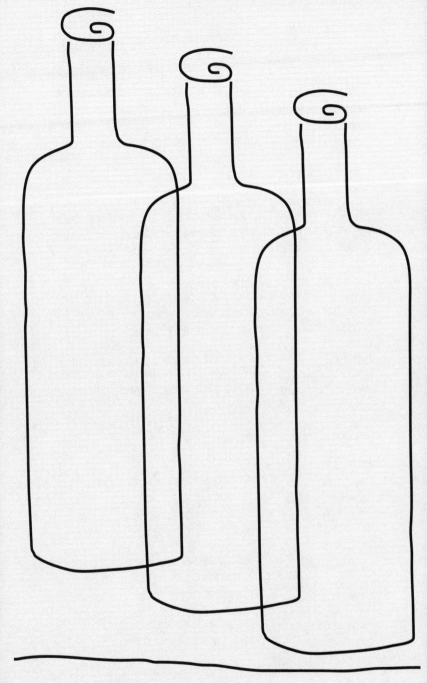

how to buy wine

Buying a bottle of wine shouldn't raise the heartbeat. Wine is fun, and strolling through your local bottle shop should be a joy. It isn't a visit to the dentist. But not everyone feels confident to strut through the liquor store like they own the joint, so we offer the following advice on how to buy wine.

Get Organized

The typical liquor store or wine shop organizes its wine by country, a helpful categorical tool if you're feeling regional, but somewhat awkward if you want a Merlot and have to run around comparing one geographical offering to another. Things can get particularly unruly if you head to an Old World section like France or Italy and are confronted with regional names emblazoned across the labels instead of grape types. Get to know where certain grapes come from, and you'll be sleuthing through the bottle aisles in no time.

GrapeWHAT

What the grape? Different grapes have different personalities. Here, in five words or so, are the typical characteristics of the most common grape varieties.

Grape	WHAT?
Whites	
Chardonnay	apple, dry, often oaked, omnipresent
Chenin Blanc	green apple, steely, good acidity
Gewürztraminer	rich but refreshing, spicy, tropical
Pinot Blanc	fresh, fruity, mild, drink young
Pinot Gris	versatile, aromatic, honey
Pinot Grigio	same grape but Italian-style and crisp
Riesling	dry to sweet, good acidity, racy
Sauvignon Blanc	gooseberry, grassy, crisp, light
Semillon	lean or luscious, tupperware, honey
Torrontés	fresh, light, dry, floral
Viognier	trendy, floral, soft but peppy

Grape	WHAT?
Reds	
Cabernet Franc	raspberry, bell pepper
Cabernet Sauvignon	king grape, tannic, full, ages well
Carmenère	herbaceous, dark fruit, unique
Gamay	cherry, medium weight
Grenache	strawberry, bit rustic, potent
Malbec	plum, powerful, tannin
Merlot	approachable, smooth, full, dark fruit
Pinotage	South Africa, berry, spice
Pinot Noir	cherry, forest floor, soft tannins
Sangiovese	cherry, earthy, good acidity
Shiraz	medium, peppery, powerful, lotsa fruit
Syrah	same grape but less fruit, more earth
Tempranillo	juicy or dense, cherry or blackberry
Zinfandel	strawberry pie, brambles, jammy

GrapeWHERE

You're in a wine shop, standing in front of the Italy section, but the label just isn't telling you anything except for a region. What happened to "Chardonnay" and "Merlot"? It's a long story, but in the meantime here's the lowdown on what grapes go into some of the wines named by place.

Grape	WHERE?
Whites	
Semillon, Sauvignon Blanc	Bordeaux, France
Chardonnay	Burgundy, France (includes Mâcon Villages)
Viognier, Roussanne, Marsanne, and others	Côtes du Rhône, France
Chardonnay, Pinot Noir, Pinot Meunier	Champagne, France

Grape	WHERE?
Reds	
Cabernet Sauvignon, Merlot, Cab Franc	Bordeaux, France
Pinot Noir	Burgundy, France
Gamay	Beaujolais, France
Syrah, Grenache, and others	Côtes du Rhône, France
Grenache, Syrah, Cinsault, Mourvèdre, Carignan	Côtes du Ventoux, France
Sangiovese	Chianti, Italy
Tempranillo, Garnacha	Rioja, Spain
Mencia	Bierzo, Spain

Occasional Wine

Of course, regardless of how the wines are organized, we're often there to buy a wine for a certain occasion, be it to go with Mom's meatloaf or to celebrate Jane's birthday. This is a logical way to buy wine, especially—excuse us—for the occasional wine drinker.

GrapeWHEN

Matching wines to food and/or occasion is like accessorizing an outfit. You want everything to go together, but that doesn't mean you have to be obvious. And there are bonus points for creativity. (See the section starting on page 32 for more hints.)

Grape	WHEN?
Whites	
Chardonnay	chicken, crab
Chenin Blanc	snapper, salad
Gewürztraminer	curry, Asian
Pinot Blanc	goat cheese, veggie soup
Pinot Gris	halibut, smoked salmon
Riesling	turkey, apple sauce
Sauvignon Blanc	shellfish, fish
Semillon	prawns, pork

Grape	WHEN?
Torrontés	aperitif, carrot soup
Viognier	grilled fish, ginger
Champagne	in the bath with mango and a friend

Reds	
Cabernet Franc	roast, goulash
Cabernet Sauvignon	steak, kebabs
Carmenère	alone, late at night
Gamay	nachos
Malbec	slow-grilled food, stuffed cabbage
Merlot	Camembert, mushrooms
Pinotage	pork, game
Pinot Noir	salmon, duck
Sangiovese	pizza, pasta
Shiraz	BBQ
Tempranillo	bacon, beef stir-fry
Zinfandel	nachos, teriyaki
Port	with a book

Feelings, Nothing More Than Feelings

There's nothing better than matching wines to mood, and often when we find ourselves staring at a wall of wine wondering what to put in the basket, a simple mood check serves to stimulate the purchase process. A bold evening often calls for an aggressive wine, just as a mellow affair requires an equally subdued bottle.

FEELING	TRY	FROM
Bold/Aggressive	Shiraz	Australia/BC
Mellow/Chill	Pinot Noir	France/California
Sophisticated	Cabernet Blend	Chile
Edgy	Riesling	Germany/Australia
Ambivalent	Chardonnay	Anywhere

Expanding Your Wine Horizons

And while we're still on the topic of feelings . . . If you're feeling a bit adventurous, it's the perfect time to experiment with a never-before-tasted wine.

LIKE	TRY	FROM
Cabernet Sauvignon	Tempranillo	Spain
Shiraz	Côtes du Rhône	France
Merlot	Malbec	Argentina
Chardonnay	Pinot Gris	BC
Sauvignon Blanc	Grüner Veltliner	Austria

Required Reading

What appears on the wine label counts—you can learn a lot about a wine before you buy. The trick is to know what's worth reading. Wine label literacy can go a long way to increasing wine enjoyment and decreasing buyer remorse.

Old World

New World

Wine or winery name
Back in the day, the name would be that of a chateau or domaine, or possibly it'd be a proprietary name that was used by a winemaking co-operative. While these are still out there, now brand names, animal species, and hip monikers are gracing wine bottles—all in an effort to help you remember what you drank.

Vintage
The year printed on the label is the year the grapes were grown. There are good years and bad years, usually determined by

weather conditions. Should you care? In good grape-weather years there'll be more good wine, but off years don't necessarily mean bad wine. If the winemakers know what they're doing, their wines should be able to overcome the less-than-perfect vintages. A vintage also tells you how old the wine is. Oldies are not necessarily goodies, but many wines will improve with cellar time (see page 28).

We include the vintages for the wines we review. Where no vintage is listed, the wine is "non vintage" meaning it's been made from a mix of years.

Alcohol

Generally expressed as "alcohol by volume" (ABV), this tells you how much wine you can taste before the line between "tasting" and "drinking" becomes blurred. Or blurry. As a rough guide, a higher alcohol content (14 percent is high, anything above 14.5 percent is really high) suggests a heftier, more intense wine. On the other side of the ABV spectrum, wines with less than 11 percent will often be off-dry (slightly sweet). High alcohol doesn't connote a better wine. Regardless of the number, if the wine is without the grating bitterness of alcohol—and not dishwater thin—then it's a well-balanced drop.

Appellation

Or, where the grapes came from. Old World wine, say from France, often gives you the appellation instead of the grape variety. You'll see something like "Bordeaux," which describes where the grapes originated, but because French laws state only certain grapes are authorized in certain areas, the appellation name also hints at what grapes made the wine. For some examples, refer to GrapeWHERE on page 21.

Grape variety

You pick up a can of soup and it's "mushroom" or "tomato." On a wine bottle it's the grape variety that defines the wine: Shiraz or Merlot or Chardonnay, to mention a few. These are your "single varietal" wines, as opposed to "blended" wines, the likes of Cabernet-Merlot and Semillon–Sauvignon Blanc. Keep in mind, single varietal wines are no better than blends and vice versa. It all comes down to good winemaking creating good-tasting wine. Trust your taste buds.

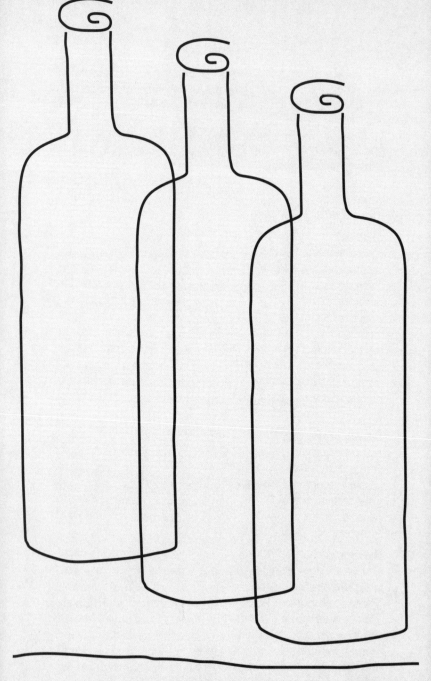

how to enjoy wine

Glasses and Stemware

Not all wineglasses are created equal, though drinking wine from any glass can be equally enjoyable. Allow us to explain.

Wine is like golf. There's an infinite array of specialized accessories, but all you really need to play the game is a set of clubs. Likewise, all your wine requires is a glass. It's up to you to decide how much you want to invest and how involved you want to get. Just don't tell us you can't drink wine because you don't have a wineglass.

There are benefits to good stemware:

- Swirling wine in the larger bowl common to fancy glasses does wonders for a wine's aromas. Pouring a few fingers at a time lets you get a proper swirl going.

- Holding the stem helps to keep white wines chilled and grubby fingerprints off the glass.

- There's no denying the elegant tactile sensation of a thin rim caressing the lips.

We use a motley collection of crystal we've collected over the years as well as a cupboard full of everyday tumblers for backyard bashes.

Decanters

After glasses and a corkscrew, the next most important wine accessory is the decanter. A secret to wine enjoyment, the decanter can do more for your wines than you'd imagine. Decanting old wines to remove the liquid from the sediment will keep your teeth clean, but how many of us drink old wines these days?

Use your decanter to decant young wines, letting them breathe. Most wines we buy are made to be drunk young—often too young—and decanting will open these wines up, revealing their character. Your decanter is a wine time machine; don't be afraid to shake it.

Anything can be used as a decanter, from a clean teapot to a water jug. To get serious about your decanter, look for a glass container with a wide base and a narrow opening. This facilitates swirling, makes for easier pouring—and looks pretty sexy.

Corkscrews

We've been to our share of dinner parties where the main event was getting the cork out of the bottle. Usually at the mercy of an antediluvian Butterfly corkscrew.

We think it would be a better wine world if everyone's knife drawer also had a Waiter's Friend. They're cheap (you can find them under $10) and effective (never yet met a cork it couldn't beat), and make you look like you mean wine business when looped around your belt.

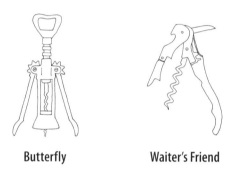

Butterfly   **Waiter's Friend**

Storing and Aging Your Wine

We don't mean to come across like we're down on wine cellars—quite the opposite. There's nothing we like better than rummaging around dusty wine racks sticky with cobwebs. But there's wine for aging and there's wine for drinking, and this book is about the latter.

In fact, over 90 percent of the wine sold today is made for drinking now, and to drink a wine now, you don't need a cellar. But, they say—and we've tasted proof—that wine changes as it gets older, hence the concept of storing wine.

Do you need a cellar or a sub-zero? For most, no. Display your wine in that IKEA wine rack, stash it in the cupboard, or keep it handy under your bed.

Wine Handling

Serving temperatures

18°C (65°F) *a bit below room temperature*	Red wine
10°C (50°F) *20 minutes out of the fridge*	White (and rosé) wine
5°C (40°F) *straight from the fridge*	Sparkling and sweet wine

Tips

- Err on the side of serving a wine too cold. The bottle will always warm up as it sits on the table.

- If you're not enjoying a wine, chill it well to mask many off-flavours.

- If a wine is too sweet, serving it cold will make it taste drier.

- All dessert wine should be served at fridge temperature, unless it's red—like port—in which case serve at the same temperature as red wine.

Leftovers

Once a bottle is opened, how long do you have to drink it? It's true that wine starts to deteriorate once it's exposed to oxygen, but finishing a bottle the following day—or if you must, even the day after—is fine.

Sure, there are tricks. Put the open bottle in the fridge, whether white or red, to slow down the oxidization, or use a vacuum pump to remove oxygen from the bottle, or buy spray bottles filled with inert gas to blanket the wine, protecting against oxygen, or drop marbles into the bottle to displace the air.

But if you ask us, you're better off breaking out a chunk of cheese and polishing off the contents.

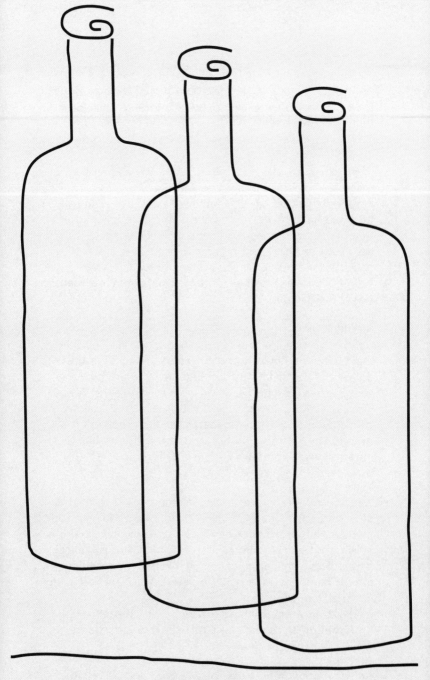

food and wine

We prepare our meals to match the wine we want to drink. We order a steak only if we feel like drinking red wine. But, we've been told, some people decide first what they're going to eat, then think about what wine to have.

Strategies

Red meat
Red wine. There are a lot of wine myths out there, and half of them are Grade "A" bull. "Red wine with red meat," however, is true. Besides synchronizing colours, red meat is hearty. It's full-flavoured and heavy, and red wines—especially Cabernets (see page 108 for a great Cab), Merlots (page 128), and Syrahs (page 120)—follow the same lines. **Strategy: match the big intensities of the flavours.**

Shellfish
Light, white wine. There are even white wines, like fino sherry, that taste briny. Could you ask for a better match? We also bet on white wines that have no, or little, oak flavour. These wines will taste fresh, just how you want your shellfish to be. Of note, Rieslings (page 58) and Sauvignon Blancs (page 77) are tangy with crisp acidity. **Strategy: match the lightness and freshness of the flavours. Bonus strategy: if there's lemon or lime involved, wine with high acidity is good.**

Salmon
Medium white or lighter red wine. "Salmon steak" should tip you off. It's fish, sure, but if you've ever had a spring salmon flopping around on the deck of your boat, you know the fish is no shrimp. Good BC salmon has plenty of flavour, and it takes a wine with extra heft to get along. White-wise, oaked or un-oaked Chardonnays (page 52). Red-wise, try a Pinot Noir (page 88 for a Dornfelder–Pinot Noir blend). And don't forget rosé (page 82). **Strategy: match a rich white with the rich omega-3s of salmon; if it's red, make sure the tannins are soft.**

White fish
Light to medium white wine. The way you cook the fish makes all the difference. Poached, go for a light wine like Chasselas (page 60) or Pinot Blanc (page 61). The delicacy of a poached

fish needs a delicate wine. Baked, opt for a bit of thickness from the same blend of a white Bordeaux (page 49) or go with a Pinot Grigio (page 67). Fried in a glorious sea of butter, open a Chardonnay (page 74) or a sparkling wine (page 139). **Strategy: the more oil, the heavier your wine can be.**

Pork
Medium to full whites; light to medium reds. The "other" white meat can take to a lot of different wines. We love a good, off-dry Gewürztraminer (page 62) if there's a German flair to your cooking (read: apple sauce); we love an Italian red (page 90) if it's a pot roast. **Strategy: you can definitely put grapes before pigs. Pork is highly wine-friendly—it's all to do with how you sauce it.**

Chicken
Medium white wine. Everyone likes chicken, right? And likewise, everyone's happy with a medium-bodied, dry white wine. How can you go wrong? This is the perfect combo to serve your date the first time you cook for them. Unless they're vegetarian. Then serve pasta alfredo. Unless they're vegan. Then serve tofu. Anyway, a Semillon blend works (page 49), and if you want to get creative, try a Grüner Veltliner (page 75). **Strategy: hard to go wrong with white wine and chicken. Can work with cream sauce or tofu as well.**

Spicy
Fruity, off-dry white wine. Putting wine against spice is like pitting the Dukes of Hazzard against the A-Team. We pity the fool! In mild doses, a slightly sweet, fruity wine like Gewürztraminer (page 64) or an aromatic white blend (page 56) will show through spice, but if it's heavy jalapeño, go beer. Heavy red wines will upper-cut your palate and you'll taste nothing but hard-hitting tannins. **Strategy: get a white wine that has more flavour than the dish has spice.**

Heavy sauce
White or medium red. We learned the definition of "heavy sauce" in Paris. Cream and butter, baby. It challenges wine-pairing because whatever you put the sauce on tastes a lot like the sauce. If it's classic roux, what works is a white like Chenin

Blanc (page 54) or a soft, medium red from Spain (page 112). **Strategy: prevent cardiac arrest with some polyphenols and a walk around the block after dinner.**

Dessert
Red or white wine that's sweeter than the dessert. If the wine is too dry, the sweet dessert will make it seem even drier, and that's just way too dry for us. Both the Tyrrell's Tawny (page 148) and the Graham's Port (page 149) are sweet but not cloying, and this is why they rock. People seem to like dry red wine with chocolate. Here, make sure your red wine is full-flavoured and not too tannic, like the Amado Sur (page 103). **Strategy: late harvest, icewine, port, sweet sherry, Madeira. This is your arsenal.**

Cheese
Try anything. It won't hurt. A wine salesperson once told us, "If you want to sell wine, serve cheese." The magical mud called cheese makes everything taste good. We highly recommend it before dinner, during dinner, and definitely after dinner. Creamy cheese is tasty with a creamy wine like the Ardèche Chardonnay (page 52), hard cheese with a solid wine like the Dehesa Gago (page 131). A beautiful match is blue cheese and dessert wine (see the chapter starting on page 146). **Strategy: we always run out of cheese, so stock up.**

Icons

These icons will reappear in our list of wines. Note that the index starting on page 155 organizes the wines in this book by food icon.

Food icons
Wine and food together is gastronomy in stereo. We list general guidelines for each wine to help your pairings sing.

BEEF
Big protein: roast, steak, stew

CHEESE
Hard or soft,
stinky or mild

CHOCOLATE
The darker the better

FISH
Trout, salmon,
halibut, tuna

LAMB
The other red meat

ON ITS OWN

PORK
Chops, kebabs,
loin

POULTRY
Turkey, chicken,
duck, guinea fowl

SHELLFISH
Bi-valves, oh my!:
oysters, mussels, clams

SPICY
Szechuan, mild curry,
Thai

VEGETARIAN
Tofu-friendly: stir-fries,
ratatouille, mushrooms galore

Occasion icon

 Wine is tied to experience. There's a wine for every occasion, but certain times call for specific wines. Whether the moment is casual or formal, serious or celebratory, a glass of wine can match the mood.

APERITIF
Suitable pre-meal to get the gastro-juices flowing

BEGINNER
Easy to drink, vari-etally true wines

BYO
Crowd-pleasers; wines to pack along

CELLAR
Wines that get better after a couple of years

PATIO/PICNIC
Hot weather sipping wines

ROCK OUT
Wines to let your hair down, tussle that do, and coif that mullet

ROMANCE
Wines to get busy with

WEDNESDAY WINE
To get you through the mid-week hump

WINE GEEK
Wines on the esoteric side that only a geek could love

WINTER WARMER
Wines to ward off any chill

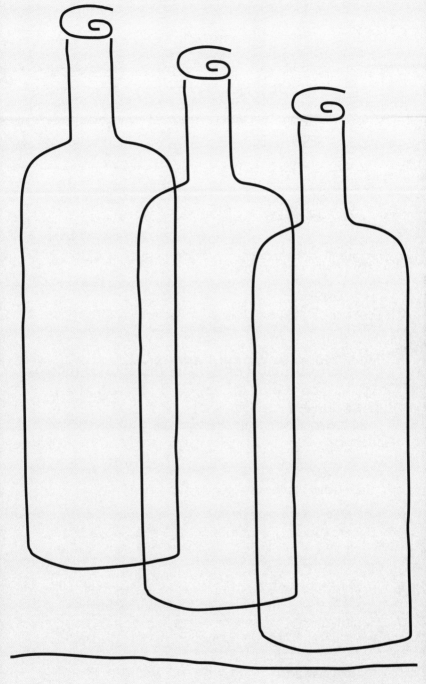

recipes

This year, we turn to the pros for recipes. We love finding inspiration among the pages of cookbooks. We've combed the Whitecap archives to select some easy, solid recipes for dishes that go great with wine. We've even provided some wine ideas to accompany each dish.

We have to admit, even as card-carrying carnivores, we've been inclined to eat less meat. We'll leave aside the ethics, environment, and health debates and instead focus on the fact that here we have a delicious, simple-to-make veggie option that is both completely satisfying and a winner with wine. We'll eat (and drink) to that!

bulgar-stuffed avocados

from V Cuisine: The Art of New Vegan Cooking

by Angeline Linardis

prep time 30 minutes | **cooking time** none | **makes** 2 servings

1 cup (250 mL)	bulgar wheat
1	red onion, finely diced
2	medium tomatoes, finely diced
¼ cup (60 mL)	finely chopped cilantro
2 Tbsp (30 mL)	extra virgin olive oil
2 Tbsp (30 mL)	fresh lemon or lime juice
	salt and pepper to taste
2	large ripe avocados

1 Place the bulgar wheat in a bowl and pour enough boiling water over it to cover, plus a little extra. Soak for about 20 minutes. Drain off all the water.

2 Combine the soaked bulgar, onion, tomatoes, and cilantro in a large bowl. Add the olive oil and lemon juice, and season with the salt and pepper.

3 Cut the avocados in half and remove the pits. Using a spoon, scoop out some of the flesh, being careful to keep it whole. Fill the avocados with the bulgar mixture. Slice the scooped out flesh and place the slices on top. Garnish with more cilantro and serve immediately.

serve: 1. Quails' Gate Chardonnay (page 70), 2. Winery of Good Hope Chenin Blanc (page 54), 3. Hungaria Brut (page 139)

Big-ups to the bottom feeders. Line-caught halibut and wild (or close-contained farmed) salmon are great, but designer fish cost big-time bucks. For more value for your omega-3 dollar, not to mention a nod to sustainable aquaculture, look instead to the underappreciated fish like sardines. When we stumbled across some plump fresh speci-mens at the fishermen's wharf, we scored ten for the price of a couple sockeye steaks. But how to cook them? Of course, way ahead of us was a whiz of a cook—and Joie Winery mastermind—Heidi Noble, with her elegantly easy version of a classic Spanish dish.

sardine escabeche

from Menus from an Orchard Table: Celebrating the Food and Wine of the Okanagan

by Heidi Noble

prep time 1 hour | **cooking time** 2 minutes | **makes** 6 servings

12	whole sardines
1 cup (250 mL)	all-purpose flour, seasoned with salt, pepper, and paprika
½ cup (125 mL)	olive oil, divided
½ cup (125 mL)	red wine vinegar
1	medium onion, thinly sliced
a 2-inch (5 cm) strip	orange zest
1 sprig	fresh thyme
1 sprig	fresh rosemary
1	fresh bay leaf
4 cloves	garlic, crushed
2	dried red chilies
1 tsp (5 mL)	salt
1 small bunch	fresh flat-leaf parsley, roughly chopped

1 Gut, scale, and remove the heads from the sardines. Dust them in the seasoned flour. Fry them in ¼ cup (60 mL) of the olive oil for 1 minute on each side. Transfer to a shallow dish.

2 In a saucepan combine the vinegar, onion, orange zest, thyme, rose-mary, bay leaf, garlic, chilies, and salt. Bring to a boil and simmer for

about 15 minutes. Add the parsley and the remaining ¼ cup (60 mL) of olive oil. Pour this hot marinade over the sardines and allow to sit until the marinade comes to room temperature.

3 To serve, remove the sardines from the marinade. To serve as a first course, place 2 sardines on a small plate with some of the pickled onions from the brine. To serve as tapas, place sardines on a platter with toothpicks.

serve: 1. Hiedler Grüner Veltliner (page 75), 2. Château la Gravette Rosé (page 81), 3. Casal Thaulero Montepulciano d'Abruzzo (page 87)

Full disclosure: we've been fans of George and Park ever since we met them years back when they opened their first Memphis Blues BBQ joint. We even asked them to cater our first book launch, for Have a Glass. *Wine, a party, and pulled pork—it was unforgettable! These guys know their BBQ, not to mention their wine. Thankfully, those not within commuting distance of Memphis Blues (or without a backyard BBQ pit) can now re-create the heavenly pulled pork.*

oven-roasted pulled pork

from Memphis Blues Barbeque House: Bringin' Southern BBQ Home
by George Siu and Park Heffelfinger

prep time 15 minutes | **cooking time** 4–4½ hours | **makes** 6 servings

1 Tbsp (15 mL)	dried parsley
1 Tbsp (15 mL)	sugar
1 Tbsp (15 mL)	Lawry's Seasoned Salt
½ tsp (2 mL)	garlic powder
½ tsp (2 mL)	onion powder
½ tsp (2 mL)	dried oregano
½ tsp (2 mL)	ground black pepper
½ tsp (2 mL)	sweet paprika
¼ tsp (1 mL)	mild mustard powder
¼ tsp (1 mL)	celery salt
large pinch	cayenne pepper
4 lb (2 kg)	boneless pork shoulder or picnic shoulder

1 Preheat the oven to 225°F (105°C).

2 Combine the dried parsley, sugar, seasoned salt, garlic powder, onion powder, dried oregano, black pepper, paprika, mustard powder, celery salt, and cayenne pepper in a small bowl. Make sure there are no clumps.

3 Rub the pork shoulder liberally with the dry rub. Place the shoulder in a roasting pan, fat cap up, and cook in the preheated oven for 3 hours. Remove from the oven, wrap with aluminum foil, and cook for another hour. Test it by pushing down on the pork shoulder. When it's done it should feel tender and ready to fall apart; if it's still too firm, cook for another 30 minutes.

4 Remove from the oven and unwrap the pork. Use 2 forks to separate the pork while it rests in the roasting pan. There will be natural juices and drippings that you can incorporate back into the pulled pork. Just massage them in with your hands (clean, of course!). This will add extra flavour and keep it nice and moist. Serve on a bun, with a salad, or as a meal. It's versatile!

serve: 1. Gabarda Cariñena (page 112), 2. The Black Chook Sparkling Shiraz (page 142), 3. St. Urbans-Hof Riesling (page 78)

There are wine-friendly recipes, and then there are recipes, like this one, that scream to have wine paired to them. Suffice it to say, this is our kind of recipe. The beef will take on nearly any full-flavoured red you throw at it, and the wild mushrooms add a flavour complexity that sings if there's a little funk in the wine. And why not try a white? Something cool and crisp can offer a palate wake-up.

beef tenderloin with wild mushrooms and leeks

from Pure Food: How to Shop, Cook and Have Fun in Your Kitchen Every Day

by Christine Cushing

prep time 10 minutes | **cooking time** 15 minutes | **makes** 4 servings

four 3 oz (90 g) rounds	beef tenderloin (each about 2 inches/5 cm thick)
to season	sea salt
to season	freshly cracked black peppercorns
2 tsp (10 mL)	Worcestershire sauce

1 Tbsp (15 mL)	chopped fresh thyme
1 Tbsp (15 mL)	grapeseed oil
2 Tbsp (30 mL)	butter
¾ cup (185 mL)	chopped wild mushrooms (try morel or shiitake)
1	small shallot, finely sliced
½	small leek, white part only, cut in half lengthwise and thinly sliced
¼ cup (60 mL)	brandy
½ cup (125 mL)	beef stock
½ cup (125 mL)	whipping cream (35%)
2 Tbsp (30 mL)	chopped fresh chives, for garnish

1 Preheat the oven to 350°F (180°C).

2 Season the beef with the salt and pepper, Worcestershire sauce, and chopped thyme. In a large skillet over high, heat the grapeseed oil until hot. Add the seasoned beef tenderloin and sear for about 1 minute per side until just browned. Transfer to a small roasting pan and roast in the oven for 6 to 8 minutes until medium rare.

3 Using the same skillet, melt the butter over medium-high heat. Add the mushrooms and sauté until golden, about 2 minutes. Add the shallot and leek and cook for a further 2 minutes until softened. Deglaze with the brandy. Add the beef stock and cream and continue cooking for 4 to 6 minutes over medium heat until the liquid has reduced and slightly thickened. Adjust the seasoning.

4 Place the meat on 4 plates. Pour the brandy-cream sauce overtop, garnish with the chives, and serve.

serve: 1. A-Mano Primitivo (page 119), 2. Saint Cosme Côtes du Rhône (page 135), 3. Summerhill Pinot Gris (page 72)

This is the simplest, most delicious pastry dessert we know. Sure, you have to get a little dirty, assembling pastry dough and making syrup. But trust us; it's so worth it. You'll get no complaints from your company when, at the end of the meal, you present this dessert and wine ambrosia. The smell of fresh baking wafting from the kitchen is never a bad thing either.

upside-down pear tart

from The Passionate Cook

by Karen Barnaby

prep time 45 minutes | **cooking time** 20–30 minutes | **makes** one 10-inch (25 cm) tart

Pastry

2 cups (500 mL)	all-purpose flour
1 Tbsp (15 mL)	sugar
¼ tsp (1 mL)	sea salt
¾ cup (185 mL)	chilled unsalted butter
⅓ cup (80 mL)	ice-cold water

Filling

8	slightly underripe Bartlett pears
½ cup (125 mL)	unsalted butter
1 cup (250 mL)	sugar

1 For the pastry, place the flour, sugar, and sea salt in a large bowl and whisk well to combine. Cut the butter into ¼-inch (6 mm) cubes and toss with the flour mixture. Add the ice-cold water all at once and blend it in with your hands. Knead gently with the tips of your fingers until the dough forms a rough ball.

2 Flatten the dough, wrap in plastic wrap, and refrigerate for 30 minutes.

3 Preheat the oven to 400°C (200°F).

4 For the filling, peel, core, and cut the pears into quarters. In a heavy skillet, melt the butter over medium heat. Add the sugar and cook, stirring frequently, until the sugar turns a deep brown. Add the pears

and cook, turning frequently. As they cook, they will shrink and exude juice that will combine with the sugar and butter to form a syrup. As each piece of pear becomes caramelized, transfer the piece, cut side down, to a deep 10-inch (25 cm) pie plate. When the pears are done, pour the syrup and any remaining pears into the pie plate.

5 On a floured surface, roll out the pastry to ¼-inch (6 mm) thickness. Cut the pastry into a circle that is 1 inch (2.5 cm) larger than the pie pan. To pick up the pastry, roll it around the rolling pin and unroll it over the pears. Tuck the edges into the pan and bake until the pastry is golden brown, about 20 to 30 minutes. Allow the tart to cool before turning it out onto a plate. Serve warm with lightly whipped cream or crème fraîche.

serve: 1. Jacob's Creek Chardonnay–Pinot Noir Brut Cuvée (page 140), 2. Château la Rame Sainte Croix du Mont (page 150), 3. St. Rémy V.S.O.P. (page 147)

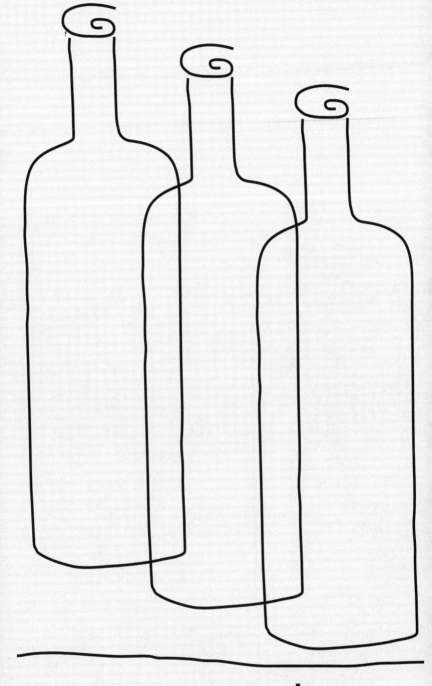

the whites

trapiche

In this red-centric wine world, not much fanfare is made over the "other" Bordeaux blend. White Bordeaux involves Semillon, Sauvignon Blanc, and sometimes a splash of Muscadelle, the resulting wine offered in diverse styles ranging from bone dry to sweet Sauternes. Halfway round the world from Bordeaux, Trapiche blends 60 percent Sauv Blanc with 40 percent Semillon to create their homage: a delightful quaffer that's a steal at nine bucks. The Sauv Blanc provides fresh, fruity lemon/lime tang and tropical pineapple while Semillon acts as smooth enforcer, offering intensity and richness. Overall, a straight-up crowd-pleaser at a refreshing price.

**2007
Sauvignon Blanc–Semillon
"Astica"
$9.00**

 clam chowder

 patio/picnic, Wednesday wine, beginner

finca los primos

Really, who doesn't like a great wine value? The label gazers can keep their precious First Growths and Super-Tuscans (though admittedly, we won't turn down a glass if offered). We'll keep hunting for fun wines that won't bust the budget. That said, quality $10 bottles appear to be headed the way of dollar-a-litre unleaded. This makes Finca Los Primos's new vintage of Chard all the more impressive. It's a solid, fresh, and easy-drinking Chardonnay that over-delivers for the price. Green apple and peach keep things fruity, while nice balance and crispness keep the palate ready for the next sip. A good everyday white, all year round.

2007

SAN RAFAEL

FINCA LOS PRIMOS

ARGENTINA

CHARDONNAY

Produced and Bottled by
VALENTIN BIANCHI SACIF
San Rafael - Mendoza
Produit d'Argentine
Product of Argentina

14 %alc./vol.   750 ml.

**2007
Chardonnay
$9.95**

turkey burgers

schnitzel

aperitif, BYO

barefoot

"Non vintage" on a table wine is typically code for dishwater plonk. When there's no year written on the bottle, the provenance of the contents likely lead to one gigantic melange of leftover grape juice. That's why we were pleasantly surprised by Barefoot's unyeared Pinot Grigio, a vibrant pear skin and apple swigger with an easygoing finish. This is fun, accessible wine at a very accessible price, a winning combo every time.

 guacamole

 rock out, beginner

Pinot Grigio
$9.99

Australia

long flat white

This is blogging wine.

You know, when it's 12:32 a.m. and you're sitting in front of your Mac with head-phones on, listening to the new Blonde Redhead, or old Blonde Redhead, or maybe Avril Lavigne. Anyway, whichever way you punk (pop- or post-), while you blog away with raillery, sip on a bottle of wine. Not just any wine, but one that's packed with lychee, rose petals, and a full-on tropical explosion. Perfect for after hours in the blogosphere.

 dolmathes

 tamales

 patio/picnic, Wednesday wine

2006
Semillon–Sauvignon Blanc
$12.99

viñedos raimat

2006
Albariño-Chardonnay
$12.99

Beauty and the geek.

Sonny and Cher. Magic Johnson and Vlade Divac on the '89–'90 Lakers. There are some pairings that at first pass don't seem like they'll work, but manage to come together into something successful. Raimat's white blend is the wine equivalent. It's not like Albariño-Chardonnay rolls off the tongue, but the austere Albariño sure balances with the smooth Chardonnay to create a fantastic fusion of apple, pear, chiramoya, and marzipan goodness that flows with richness and ends with a crisp, bright finish.

 coconut prawns

 roast chicken

 wine geek, rock out, romance

Chile

concha y toro

Straight up and straight down is the only way we like our Chardonnay. Forget the funny business of lathering the grape variety in oak, or even worse, jumping in fully unwooded, only to muddle it with winemaker tricks. Straight up means the Chardonnay is one of two ways: good-quality fruit kissed with some spiced wood, or sans tree but not afraid to go dry and crisp. Concha y Toro's Casillero del Diablo is the essence of balance, hooking up tasty, appley fruit with a pinch of vanilla smoki-ness. Whether they use real barrels or oak "technologies" (i.e., wood chips) we're not fussy: this drop goes straight down with no complaints.

 yakitori

 beginner, romance

2007
Chardonnay
"Casillero del Diablo"
$13.00

louis latour

If the best Chardonnay is grown on the rolling hillsides of Burgundy, then the best value Chardonnay is grown in a lesser-known appellation in the Rhône called Ardèche. Forget the Grand Crus, the Premier Crus, and even those showy Bourgognes. From some 70 kilometres south of top-dollar Chardonnay, comes some serious Franco value. Fine apple flavours tweaked by a spicy note will have you thinking, "I can't believe it's not Burgundy."

 cioppino

 fish n' chips

 Wednesday wine, beginner

2005
Chardonnay
"Ardèche"
$13.49

France

paul mas

It was in Japan where we first tried a bottle of Paul Mas Viognier. There it's legal to drink in public places. You can uncork that bottle of P. M. in the middle of Shinjuku as you admire the cherry blossoms, sip with the rich of Roppongi Hills, or swirl while sitting on the steps of the Meiji Jingu Shrine—and you won't get arrested. You might get a sideways glance from 12 million people, but you won't get cuffed. With its luscious aromas of ginger, spice, and nutmeg, this Paul Mas pairs perfectly with the feverish buzz of any metropolis.

 on its own

 tempura

 patio/picnic, Wednesday wine

2006
Viognier
$13.99

winery of good hope

Give Chenin a chance!

You may have heard us decry the dearth of potable Chenin Blanc available locally, and as the scene hasn't changed much it's worth revisiting. When handled correctly, the grape makes an amazingly versatile white wine that has serious potential to evolve gracefully in the cellar. One of the better, not to mention superb value, options right now is this honest offering from the Winery of Good Hope, filled with full-on fresh melon and honeyed goodness that are hallmarks of classy Chenin.

WINE OF SOUTH AFRICA

THE WINERY OF GOOD HOPE

The first Cape wine flowed in 1659

CHENIN BLANC

2007
Chenin Blanc
$13.99

 halibut cheeks

 prosciutto-wrapped melon

 patio/picnic, wine geek

Chile

cono sur

Cono Sur
Chardonnay
Colchagua Valley
CHILE
Product of Chile
White Wine
13% alc./vol.
Produit du Chili
Vin Blanc
750 ml
Wine made from grapes in conversion to organic agriculture

**If Cono Sur made a
hundred different
wines, this book would
write itself.** With every cork we
pull—or every cap we unscrew—from
this Chilean winery, we are increasingly impressed. Maybe it's because the southern
hemisphere is six months ahead, but when
we were loving Viognier a few years back,
they delivered. When we started thinking
greener, they gave us an organic line of
wines. This year, we're thinking classic cuts
without the bourgeois price tag—and
here's a spitting image of mouth-watering
Mâcon (fresh, green apple, mineral) that
you can afford to gulp.

 chowder

 Thai

 winter warmer, BYO

2007
Chardonnay
$14.49

d'arenberg

2006
"Stump Jump White"
$14.99

Admittedly, the Stump Jump label is quite verbose. But we'll take text over animal pictures any day, especially when it's a nice, strong—and easy-to-read—serif font. We suggest pouring a glass of this unoaked, crisp, yet rich Riesling, Sauvignon Blanc, Roussanne, and Marsanne blend while you pore over the bottle. That way you'll learn about the fascinating origins of the "stump jump" plow. If this fruity, fun white blend hasn't got you up and mingling by the second glass then something is seriously wrong.

 on its own

 green curry

 patio/picnic, Wednesday wine

tormaresca

James is a "yellow," Kenji's a "blue"—you know, based on those personality tests that determine your colour energy. This cheery, well-made Chard appeals across the spectrum, satisfying Kenji's analytical, questioning palate while oozing character to quench James's thirsty soul. Actually, it would probably appeal to the "greens" and "reds" out there too.

 Japanese croquettes

 BLT sandwiches

 BYO, aperitif

2005 Chardonnay $14.99

wolf blass

YELLOW LABEL

South Australia
RIESLING
2006

...of great character and distinction from South Au...
...à les origines d'Australie du Sud alliant caractère et or...

WHITE WINE · VIN BLANC
PRODUCT OF AUSTRALIA · PRODUIT D'AUSTRALIE

**2006
Riesling
$15.00**

This wine isn't for everyone. But we think everyone should taste it. At least once. Riesling is the unsung superstar of diversity in the white wine world, marking a miscellany of sensory enjoyment that would make Stevie Wonder sound like Muzak. For Riesling, the variation is not so much about the decade as the variety of vinous results by geographic birthplace: Germany, France, or Australia to name a few. With this bottle, Wolf Blass treats us to a taste of Aussie Riesling, dry and austere, with plenty of diesel and lime rind notes. That's right, diesel never tasted this good.

 on its own

 spiced-up curry

 aperitif, wine geek

France

brumont

This wine was born with a silver spoon in its neck. It's always good news when Alain Brumont is pushing the buttons. He's the man of Madiran, a lesser-known patch of dirt in southwest France. Brumont's claim to fame is putting the Gascogne on the wine map, by making some stellar swill out of Tannat (a red wine labelled as Madiran) and Gros Manseng (here blended with Sauvignon Blanc).

 sole with tomato sauce and pasta

 on its own

 winter warmer, BYO

**2006
Gros Manseng–Sauvignon
$15.99**

st. hubertus

2006
Chasselas
$15.99

Vineyard hopping in northern Italy, we realized we were so close to Switzerland that we couldn't *not* see what was fermenting in the Cantons. Through the border checkpoint, we hit the first shop we found and dropped our Euros on two bottles of Chasselas, the Swiss equivalent of Pinot Blanc. The wine was good—fresh and zesty—but the stuff was so freaking expensive that we did a U-turn back to Barolo. St. Hubertus's Chasselas makes us nostalgic for that ephemeral Swiss nectar, but buying the BC version won't break our banks.

 steamed clams

 patio/picnic, aperitif

 British Columbia

red rooster

Dig the new look. Red Rooster's new labels are quite snazzy, no doubt about it. Simple and modern, the bottle should satisfy the BYOB requirements of even your most fastidious design-conscious friend. And the tart green apple and grassy stylings of this lean Pinot Blanc solidify its reputation for a safe bottle to bring along. It will please crowds and ably pull off wine duty through appetizers and the first course.

    Camembert

    on its own

    BYO, Wednesday wine

2007
Pinot Blanc
$16.99

see ya later ranch

**2006
Gewürztraminer
$16.99**

If there is one BC grape we should flaunt, our vote goes to Gewürztraminer. Not only because Gewürztraminer is such a flauntable grape—its lychee, rose petal personality is nothing short of unmistakable—but our BC soil and sunshine have a knack for ripening some top tasting Gewürz. At its best, it comes out bursting with floral and tropical aromas, an alluring oiliness, and a spicy exclamation in the finish. See Ya Later struts the stuff with this arrestingly delicious translation of the grape that shows off the Gewürz at its greatest.

 manchego

 on its own

 romance, BYO

South Africa

teddy hall

Is it just us or is an acerbic tongue a turn-on? Nothing like witty words to keep you on your feet. We also warm to soothing dialogue, so at the end of the day balance is a good thing. Sorta like this Teddy Hall Chenin. Nice depth and intensity of lime rind and pear pith, complemented by an angular herbaceousness and a honeyed finish. We could find some smarmy remark for the cheesy "summer moments" emblazoned across the front label, but with age comes maturity. We'll just pour another glass instead.

 prawn salad rolls

 Baby Belle

 beginner, cellar

**2007
Chenin Blanc
$16.99**

valckenberg

**2006
Gewürztraminer
$17.75**

Some labels are just so now. Check the bright blue and neon green on the Valckenberg: a bold and electric combination that fits right in with the fashion palette of the current crop of genre blending, electronic beat making, punk guitar riffing, New Wave synthing sensibilities of cool music groups (see Santogold, M83, and Cut Copy). Fashionable palates should gravitate to Gewürztraminer, a wine that similarly manages to blend amazing aromas with rich mouth feel in styles that cover a huge spectrum. This Valckenberg is a total rose petal potpourri bomb, super smooth and honeyed in a style that is off-dry and luscious.

 chicken karaage

 Thai curry

 patio/picnic, rock out

cline

The globalization of wine is in full effect. Feet planted in the wine aisle, we can grab great juice from New Zealand (pages 77, 82, and 127), Greece (page 69), and for the first time this year, Israel (page 122). The other aspect of wine globalization has to do with taste. Jonathan Nossiter's doc *Mondovino* (2004) pointed a few fingers at European wineries that were morphing their products to please the New World palate. OK, so Mondo rang a lot of false alarms, but after the smokescreen cleared and the wine world went back to normal, we revisited another globalization pleasantry: New World wines that tasted like European wines. Enter Cline's Viognier.

 on its own

 smokies

 romance, rock out

VIOGNIER

CLINE

2006
Viognier
$17.99

cousiño macul

2006
Sauvignon Gris
$17.99

That this wine exists is shocking. Like water and taurine (i.e., Red Bull), the concept of a Sauvignon Gris has us scratching our heads. Not that you couldn't find Sauvignon Gris before; it's just that no one cared to put it in a bottle. In the past, the grape mutation would be blended in Bordeaux, bound for appellation obscurity, but here Cousiño Macul has gone Gris point-blank. Lots of mouth-watering fruit with a citrus bang. More thirst quenching than water. Classier than a Jägerbomb.

 noodles

 grilled scallops

 wine geek, BYO

Italy

di lenardo

Pinot Grigio is all over the map. Literally. What country doesn't have a winery that labels Pinot Gris as "Grigio"? OK, France might be holding out, but the way Grigio groupies are multiplying, we might even see an Alsatian Grigio one day. Stylistically, Grigio is all over the map, too. In northern Italy—Friuli to be precise—Grigio is a serious sipping wine. Di Lenardo demonstrates what real good Grigio can be: tons of honey, apple, and peach flavours. Fresh and vibrant, with a richness needed in the global Grigio game.

 deep-fried prawns

 chicken cacciatore

 wine geek, romance

ESTABLISHED 1878 · FRIULI · ITALY

di Lenardo

VINEYARDS

PINOT GRIGIO

DAL VIGNETO VIGNE DAI VIERIS

**2006
Pinot Grigio
$17.99**

donnafugata

It's hard to "taste" this wine. It's the sort of wine that's just so sumptuous, right from the first kiss on the lips that's so good you don't want to bother taking tasting notes or dealing with any other formalities. You just want to drink it up! Peach, heather, and a multitude of other aromas and flavours ooze from this complex, lush Sicilian white. Excuse us; our glasses are waiting.

 lobster thermidor

 grilled loin

 wine geek, romance, BYO

2007
Sicilia
"Anthìlia"
$17.99

Greece

boutari

Next up: *Had a Glass's* **top 100 grapes you've never heard of.** What with all the Mencia (page 129), the Mataro (page 85), and the Zweigelt (page 137), we nearly had to rename this year's edition. Here's another from the bizarre bunch. If Moschofilero isn't in your wine-tasting lexicon, Boutari's rendition of the Greek grape will put it at the forefront of your sensory database. Loads of perfumed aromas. Loads of wine tasting fun.

 grilled sardines

 mabo tofu

 wine geek, patio/picnic

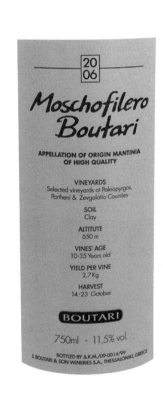

2006
Moschofilero
$18.96

quails' gate

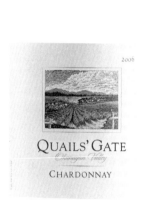

QUAILS' GATE

CHARDONNAY

**2006
Chardonnay
$18.99**

Yet more proof of white wine greatness from our backyard. Sure, BC makes some nice red wine—nice like chicken noodle soup or a sitcom plot—but pitting grape against grape, our white wines shine. And Chardonnay is always a finalist. Sorry ABC-ers, keep sipping that Sauvignon, but we think Chard has got the legs. Quails' Gate's U-20 bottling is yet more vinous proof of how great sans skins can be. Flavourful and elegant in the same sip, it'll go head-to-head with global Chard any day.

 baked quail

 risotto

 romance, BYO

South Africa

saxenburg

In the throes of winter,
when the lack of light and reliance on
wool are weighing heavy on our souls
(and our heating bills), we like to picture
an open field in full spring bloom, lush
carpets of green rolling on as far as the eye
can see. Tasting this wine transported us
there—wondrous aromas of grass, hay,
and chalk lending to a zippy but smooth,
finely balanced bottle.

 lemon grass chicken

 on its own

 aperitif, beginner

2007
"Guinea Fowl"
$18.99

summerhill

**2006
Pinot Gris
$19.95**

Despite the ocean of Pinot Gris planted in the Okanagan Valley—the hillsides, the flats, the valley floors abound with vine—there is not a lot of drop-dead delicious Gris to sip from. Why? The grapes are tasty enough—many of the vines have been in the ground since before we had licence to swirl. And local wineries have had ample chance to perfect it—the Okanagan is home to over 500 acres of the stuff. So where's the fermented disconnect? While we search for an answer, sip this Gris from Summerhill. It's a knockout for under $20.

 mild curry

 grilled mackerel

 patio/picnic

chanson

It's been a while since we've set foot in the vineyards of the Mâcon. Five years and counting since we plodded through the muddy fields, our shoes sinking into the boggy vineyard rows, as the September rain soaked us. We still have a distinct soft spot for this brisk Chardonnay wine, perhaps something to do with spending two weeks harvesting the tow-coloured grapes. Mâcon wine is a paragon that should be experienced by all (hands-on *vendange*-style, or vicariously through swirling and sniffing), and here Chanson delivers a classic, straight-up apple and citrus elixir.

 mussels and frites

 coq au vin

 wine geek, BYO

2005
Mâcon Villages
$19.99

golden mile cellars

From behind the moat, drawbridge, iron gate, and behemoth oak doors of the so-kitsch-it's-cool Golden Mile castle, comes the finest BC Chard south of $20.

Maybe the hot oil and red dragons are there to protect the top-secret recipe for wizardry winemaking. Or maybe it's to lay waste to the Philadelphia Flyers. In truth, winemaker and Habs fan, Michael Bartier, guards no secrets about how to craft lip-smacking Chardonnay—it's top-notch grapes and some cellar smarts—but seeing just how good this apple-melon-butterscotch delight is, we still think he's got a dagger or two up his sleeve.

**2006
Chardonnay
$19.99**

 Cornish game hen

 BYO, cellar

hiedler

While every mini-bar in Austria comes stocked with a bottle (albeit 200 millilitres) of Grüner Veltliner, in Canada we're lucky if we find a Chardonnay, but mostly get a Molson. Grüner is nothing short of being the signature grape of the Österreich, the hills of Lower Austria. The Grüner trend watch shows the wine has all but fallen off the vinous hot list—the Forbes 100 of fermentations. What was once "GruVee" has now been downgraded to "OutGru." But forget fashion. We'll stock our mini-bar with a Grüner Veltliner any day. The crisp, refreshing citrus bite provides endless enjoyment with or without food.

 sausages

 patio/picnic, aperitif

2005
Grüner Veltliner
$19.99

pierre sparr

A piece of relationship advice: say sorry with Gewürztraminer. Speaking from experience, it's hard to stay mad when presented with a Gewürz. It's just, well, it's tough not to get swept up by the fabulously floral and honeyed aromatics, not to mention the baked pear flavours, of a rich, lush, and amazingly textured golden Gewürztraminer like Pierre Sparr. Make wine, not war, we say!

 on its own

 stuffed eggplant

 romance, BYO, winter warmer

2006
Gewürztraminer
$19.99

New Zealand

shepherds ridge

All the grass, gooseberries, and asparagus in the world can't come close to the aromatic onslaught of some New Zealand Sauvignon Blancs. But frankly the old olfactory glands are getting a little tired of it. We wonder, are the Kiwis getting tired of it too? Our wine conspiracy theorists profess that there's New Zealand S. B. for export, and a different tank for domestic consumption. We'll happily sip some Shepherds Ridge, a bottle that blends the best of both pasture and pleasure. Everything you love about NZ S. B. is in this bottle. Chlorophyll is not.

 on its own

 patio/picnic

2007
Sauvignon Blanc
$19.99

st. urbans-hof

**2006
Riesling
Mosel Saar Ruwer
$19.99**

Goth wine at its finest.

We mean that literally. This is one Gothic beauty that epitomizes the exuberance of top-notch German Riesling. Of course, this could also be taken stylistically: the phantasmagoric black label screams gothic sensibilities. Whether you're looking for a fashion statement or a fine bottle of wine (or both), St. Urbans-Hof delivers. Lime rind, apples, slate, and an impeccable balance between sweet and sour vault this white into mythic territory.

 clam chowder

 chili garlic crab

 roast turkey

 cellar, rock out

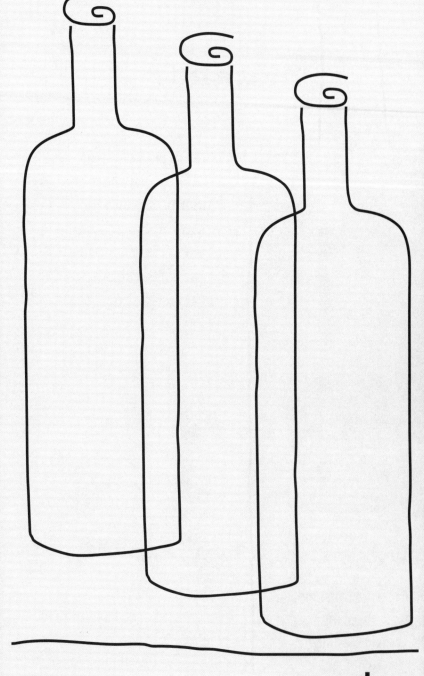

the pinks

morandé

When they told you to "drink pink" they probably weren't talking about Morandé.

They were probably talking about trash pink (punk chic Hollywood) or Shinjuku pink (tuck jeans into pink Cons). Morandé is neither. Morandé is world domination pink. The hue you need when you are planning to take control.

 California rolls

 chicken karaage

 aperitif, patio/picnic

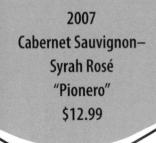

**2007
Cabernet Sauvignon–
Syrah Rosé
"Pionero"
$12.99**

château la gravette

Rosé remains our go-to summer wine choice. It's versatile, fun to drink, and aesthetically pleasing (think shades of sunset in the glass). We'd merrily sip pink wines all year, but they scream association with warm weather and long daylight hours. Plus the selection tends to be best in months without an *r.* If you're heading to a BBQ but don't know what's on the menu, think pink. And if your friends aren't hip to rosé, do them a favour and show up with a bottle of La Gravette. Classic raspberry and strawberry aromas lead to a velvety yet fresh wine; it's rich enough to stand up to a steak, but fresh enough to pair with fish.

 grilled whole trout

 rib-eye

 patio/picnic, romance, BYO

2007
Rosé
Minervois
$13.99

oyster bay

We've been known to roll out the rosés and extol their vinous virtue. Thankfully, it seems the pandering is starting to work. Rosé sales are up, and more pink wine is trickling onto our shelves. Not convinced yet? This is rosé for the red wine drinker just testing the pink wine waters. Made from Merlot, it's nice and rich and still a fruit bomb bursting with cranberry and spices. With the bonus of being fresh and vibrant, it's just the ticket for summer, patios, and any food you can throw at it.

 tacos

 Peking duck

 patio/picnic, aperitif

2007
Merlot Rosé
$17.99

segura viudas

This is how to get the party started. Nobody can refuse a cool, crisp glass of pink bubbly. Lavit not only lives up to the aesthetics, it drops some first-rate flavour, too, like a blender full of frozen field berries and orange citrus. If you're thinking strawberry daiquiri, we say, check that Miami Vice, this is Spanish Fly.

 on its own

 BYO, romance

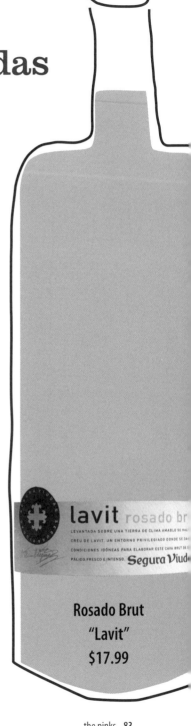

**Rosado Brut
"Lavit"
$17.99**

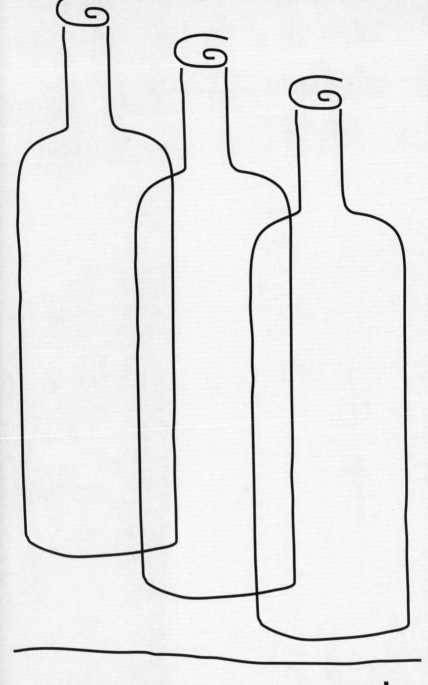

the reds

Australia

banrock station

Flavour flashback! We hadn't downed a bottle of Banrock's Shiraz-Mataro for ages, probably not since college days. Though back then it was probably something in the order of two or three bottles and an equal number of frozen pizzas. Flashback for sure. But whaddya know, Banrock's blend of Shiraz and Mataro (*Mourvèdre* if you prefer French) is still cramming the flavour of blueberries and black pepper into a drop worth studying.

 on its own

 lasagna

 BYO, Wednesday wine

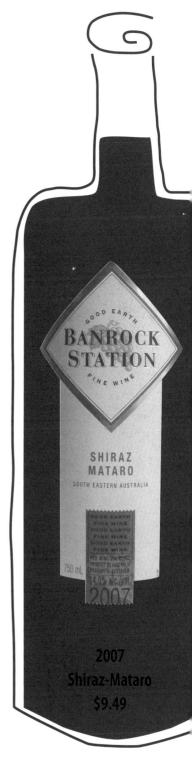

2007
Shiraz-Mataro
$9.49

terra andina

This is a wine security blanket. We take comfort knowing that we can still get straight-up tasty Chilean red for south of ten bucks. Cabernet plus Merlot—why mess with a good thing? Soft, fruity, and approachable, Terra Andina has all the qualities we look for in a go-to table red. When we're tasked with sating a crowd, we're content knowing we can turn to this warming red blend.

 turkey pot pie

 dumplings

 BYO, Wednesday wine

CHILE

TERRA ANDINA

CABERNET-MERLOT

2006

VALLE CENTRAL

Vin Rouge ~ Produit du Chili
Red Wine ~ Product of Chile

2006
Cabernet-Merlot
$9.50

Italy

casal thaulero

The full Monte. This wine doesn't shy away. It lets all its plum and black cherry hang out proudly, and there's lots there, including ripe fruit and a soft finish in a wine with surprisingly nice intensity for carrying such a thrifty price. And really this is what everyday Montepulciano d'Abruzzo is all about: gobs of fleshy, full frontal flavour that says drink me up without taking me too seriously.

 on its own

 stew

 Wednesday wine, romance

2006
Montepulciano d'Abruzzo
$9.90

st. ursula

**2006
Dornfelder–Pinot Noir
"Goldener Oktober"
$9.99**

We're not going to lie.

You'll likely get a ribbing for showing up with this bottle. Dornfelder is not the hippest grape out there and is unlikely to ever win a popularity contest. After all it's a German hybrid, crossing Helfensteiner and Heroldrebe. But—who cares? St. Ursula blends in Pinot Noir to up the class factor, slaps on the coolest label ever, and lets the funk and bruised cherry stylings strut in this smoothly nerdy wine.

 pastrami on rye

 paneer pakora

 wine geek, Wednesday wine, patio/picnic

josé maria da fonseca

In the World Series of Wine Poker, taste always trumps image.

First take: sniff for clues. If your opponent smells a little green, she might be holding some tough tannins. Too portly? His hand might be lacking structure. Beware of tilt: don't let an inky colour or long legs fool you. Chip management: flavour out of the gate could mean little left for the finishing rounds. Finally the math: if Periquita's at the table forget pot odds, this $11 player holds the nut hand.

 rotisserie chicken

 stew

 patio/picnic, rock out

PERIQUITA

2005

AZEITÃO · PORTUGAL

JOSE MARIA DA FONSECA

2005
Periquita
$10.99

montalto

2006
Nero d'Avola–
Cabernet Sauvignon
$11.98

Wining on a budget in Italy is no hardship.

Every cobblestone street corner you turn, there's a perfectly palatable bottle of *rosso* waiting to be liberated. OK, so if you dip too low, you'll pay the price, but we're talking quality quaffing on five Euros a day. But, we're not in Italy. We're not even rockin' in the free wine world. We're standing in the liquor store, staring at a legion of overpriced $12 shots in the dark. This is when, like in the movies, that all-too-serendipitous ray of light glances through the security glass to illuminate a bottle of Montalto. It's cheap. It's good. It's calling to you.

 mushroom ragout

 pork and beans

 rock out, winter warmer

Italy

caldora

Pop is good because it's catchy. Or, at least good pop is catchy. And it's not intended to be complicated. Perfectly fine to get caught up in the sweet sincerity and simple earnestness of pop. Caldora is pop wine. Super fruity and fragrant, straight-up ready to drink, and supreme value. Cheerful and crowd pleasing, this bottle fulfills its wine role with nary a precious, complicated riff.

 salami plate

 antipasti

 Wednesday wine, BYO

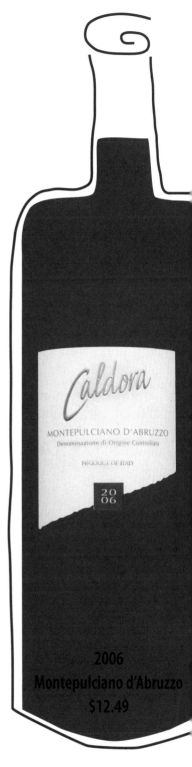

**2006
Montepulciano d'Abruzzo
$12.49**

flaio

Primitivo in southern Italy is like indie bands on the Billboard Hot 100. There are lots of them. And lots knocking on the door of mainstream. The difference is, while the guitar riffs aren't getting any better, the juice has never been tastier. With the once alternative grape finding loads of play this side of the pond, licks like this Flaio are taking the stage, rocking the one-two flavour-value chord, and our taste buds are hitting the dance floor.

 spaghetti Bolognese

 grilled mushroom caps

 rock out, beginner

Flaio

Primitivo

SALENTO

2005

750 ml ℮ RED WINE/VIN ROUGE 13.5% alc/vol
BOTTLED BY - MIS EN BOUTEILLE PAR
S.C. SPA - QUINZANO - ITALY
PRODUCT OF ITALY PRODUIT D'ITALIE

2005
Primitivo
$12.85

Chile

anakena

What's a baseball steak?

We see it on the menu sometimes, with or without sauce, charcoal or pan seared. Sounds tasty enough, but where does baseball come in to the picture? Is it the official steak of MLB? The dietary requirement of the DH? Or one you throw on the BBQ to watch the game? Anyway, regardless of what exactly baseball steak is, we think Anakena's Carmenère, a decisively brooding mouthful of big fruit flavour, goes especially well with red meat and tastes even better when the Jays are hosting—not to mention thumping—the Bo Sox.

 baseball

 BYO, beginner

2006
Carmenère
$12.95

golden kaan

Isn't Kaan the Dark Lord of the Sith? Maybe we just read too many Star Wars books, not to mention collected all the necessary action figures. So when we noticed the Kaan on the shelf, we couldn't help but get it to sip while we RPG-ed. The wine was stellar. Then we dressed up and hit the convention.

 on its own

 leg

 wine geek

2006
Shiraz
$12.99

château haut perthus

Bergerac is all about big wines and a big nose. The latter belonged, of course, to Cyrano de Bergerac, the renowned swordsman and writer who reputedly was quite proud of his proboscis. Château Haut Perthus should be proud of their latest offering, a 60/40 Cabernet Franc and Merlot blend that showcases France's warm, highly regarded 2005 vintage. Plummy and smooth, this Bergerac makes for very easy drinking and offers a great budget alternative to neighbouring—and more prominent—Bordeaux.

 Morbier

 liver and onions

 wine geek, winter warmer

2005
Bergerac
$13.95

chat-en-oeuf

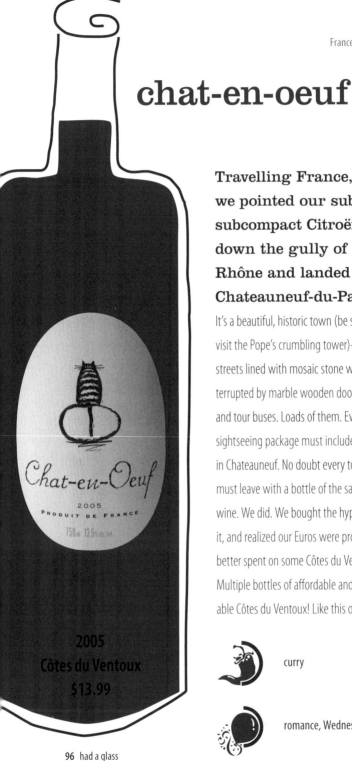

Travelling France, we pointed our sub-subcompact Citroën down the gully of the Rhône and landed in Chateauneuf-du-Pape.

It's a beautiful, historic town (be sure to visit the Pope's crumbling tower)—the streets lined with mosaic stone walls interrupted by marble wooden doorways . . . and tour buses. Loads of them. Every sightseeing package must include a stop in Chateauneuf. No doubt every tourist must leave with a bottle of the sacred wine. We did. We bought the hype. Drank it, and realized our Euros were probably better spent on some Côtes du Ventoux. Multiple bottles of affordable and quaffable Côtes du Ventoux! Like this one.

2005
Côtes du Ventoux
$13.99

 curry

 romance, Wednesday wine

Australia

thirsty lizard

We have no qualms drinking wine from a glorified cardboard box. But the goofy lizard cavorting on sun-scorched earth? Why go there? We'd love to see elegant wine Tetra Paks, not cartoons or overworked marketing concepts, because honestly the wine inside is downright enjoyable. Good depth of fruit, nice Shiraz spice, and easy-drinking balance—everything a punter could ask for at $14 a litre. We'll be camping with this portable potable all year long.

 on its own

 cheddar

 koftas

 aperitif, Wednesday wine

**2005
Shiraz
$13.99
(1-litre Tetra Pak)**

folonari

FOLONARI

VALPOLICELLA
Denominazione di
Origine Controllata

2006
Since 1825

PRODUCT OF ITALY
PRODUIT D'ITALIE
RED WINE
VIN ROUGE

12% alc./vol.   750 ml

2006
Valpolicella
$14.98

We fully support the gritty rock revival. Seems like there's been a slew of energetic groups stripping back to bare guitar and drums, leaning in heavy on the mic with punchy lyrics. Witness the revival of skinny jeans, Vans, and Ray-Bans, and we salute these bands with Valpolicella, its zippy sour cherry and easy-drinking style the epitome of pep and "come what may."

 on its own

 pizza

 rock out, romance

South Africa

beyerskloof

How cool would it be to create your own grape?

That's what A. I. Perold did in 1925, when he crossed Pinot Noir and Cinsault at Stellenbosch University and created South Africa's unique, hardy red. True, Pinotage may not have exactly taken the grape world by storm, but we maintain a soft spot for well-made, bold, and characteristic bottles. Beyerskloof is a passionate Pinotage producer, and their latest vintage—finally under screw cap—is a gangbuster of soft blackberry, plum, and black licorice playing into a cedar sawdust and smoky, almost rubbery, finish.

 anything BBQ'd

 roast squash

 wine geek, winter warmer

2006
Pinotage
$14.99

espelt

**2006
Garnacha-Cariñena
"Sauló"
$14.99**

We like it when wines taste of "somewhere."

Essentially, we're talking about wines showcasing unique character that goes with unique locale. Espelt is a ruggedly handsome wine (with an endearingly cute label) that speaks well of Empordá, the D.O. in the northern reaches of wild and rocky Catalonia, where the Pyrenees mountain range reaches out to the Mediterranean Sea and grapevines struggle in the local Sauló, or sandy gravel. A gutsy 60 percent Garnacha and 40 percent Cariñena blend, this wine is a juicy mouthful of plum and dried strawberry with a tart and tangy finish.

 on its own

 nachos

 wine geek

South Africa

kwv

This is the one bottle that was guaranteed to always be on the dinner table anytime the fam got together for a feed.

Everyone would go on about its balance, its earthiness, and its savoury qualities. Indeed, the collective family palate was right, but growing up, we just liked it for its name. Whatever makes you sip it, the Roode, the Rooder, the Roode Burger belongs on every dinner table at every family get-together. It's massively drinkable, impressively affordable, and quite the sight when everyone—including gramps—starts chanting for it in chorus.

 BBQ

 Saint-Nectaire

 Wednesday wine, BYO

2005
Roodeberg
$14.99

louis bernard

2006
Cotes du Rhône
$14.99

Here's an accessible way to get to know Côtes du Rhône. France's Rhône Valley is one of our favourite wine regions, but it's also one of the country's largest and most complicated, with a myriad of demarcations and appellations that can seem overwhelming for the novice palate. Start with this bottle. It will lay the foundation. Sixty-five percent Grenache, 35 percent Syrah, and nothing but herbs, baked earth, plum, and aromatic orange peel goodness that are the hallmarks of the invigorating wines of this region. If you enjoy it like we think you will, then start delving into the Villages, Rasteau, Gigondas, and so on.

 duck à l'orange

 Red Leicester

 beginner, rock out

trivento

Hands down, our favourite steakhouse in the world is Desnivel in Buenos Aires. This San Telmo institution isn't fancy. It isn't formal either, but you can tell it's all business the moment you walk in past the massive, hardwood, charcoal-fuelled grills manned by serious, tong-wielding tough guys. The steaks are thick and fatty; the sausages define succulent. Washing it all down is hearty red served from ceramic penguin carafes. Oh yeah, *los penguinos*! Red like the Amado Sur, an assertive Malbec, Syrah, and Bonarda blend that oozes coffee bean, plum, and smoked bacon. Rich and boisterous without busting out the seams, this is instant gratification wine at its finest.

 grilled rib-eye

 Wednesday wine, beginner

2006
Malbec-Syrah-Bonarda
"Amado Sur"
$15.00

luzón

Pulling the cork on the Luzón, you'd think suddenly a blacktop crew had set up outside your window. Welcome to Spanish garrigue. Big whiffs of tar waft from the glass, a character we find more often than not in the ripe Monastrells (Mourvèdres) of the Mediterranean. It can be quite the litmus test for wine tasting, a love it or leave it sort of thing, dependent on the individual taster's threshold for roadwork. What separates the Luzón from your average thoroughfare is its underlying juicy demeanour, balancing the package with ample plum and dark fruit flavours.

 chili

 winter warmer, BYO

2006
Jumilla
$15.45

Australia

lindemans

In the sea of "value priced" Aussie Shiraz, this bottle stands out.

Lindemans's Bin series (e.g., Bin 50 Shiraz) have long been crowd favourites, but we encourage laying out the extra couple bucks for the Reserve Shiraz. You'll still get the easy-to-love rich raspberry and blackberry plus pepper spice, but it's the fab savoury character of smoked bacon that adds an entirely new dimension. Big without being flabby, punchy without running roughshod over the taste buds. Just solid New World Shiraz.

 Parmesan

 chili beef

 rock out, winter warmer

**2005
Shiraz
"Reserve"
$15.49**

azul

In the quest to get familiar with unique, indigenous grapes, our taste buds were a-twitter when we came across the Azul. Baga! It's not every day you come across this quirky Portuguese grape, a star in the western wine region of Bairrada. Baga's full-character, thick-skinned, high-tannin, and high-acid disposition has a cult following, with fans claiming it produces wines that age like fine Bordeaux. In the Azul, Baga is blended with other Portuguese grape notables to create a rich, full-bodied wine brimming with blackberry, chocolate, and violet, capped off by a smooth, lingering finish.

pork and clams

cellar, romance

2004
Bairrada
$15.99

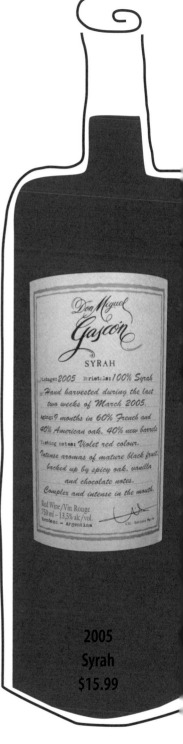

Argentina

don miguel gascón

Dust off the decanter— Gascón serves up a stinker of a Syrah. We favour using a glass carafe that we found in a dollar store, but anything will do, from one of those bulbous crystal numbers to a water pitcher. Dumping the Gascón into the carafe—and by "dump" we mean don't be timid when inverting the bottle of wine, splash it around with abandon—we kept tabs on its progress. At the two-hour mark, it had done an olfactory 180, dropping most of its earthy compost aromas for a juicy, spicy, and chocolate-covered character.

brisket

lentils with Italian sausage

wine geek, winter warmer

2005 Syrah $15.99

the reds **107**

excelsior

Does anyone make fruitcake anymore? Or even eat it? Still, fruitcake was what we were thinking about as we drank this wine, with all its comforting candied fruit, molasses, and booze. This Cab Sauv is wine fruitcake, very easy to get into and comfortingly rich and smooth.

 Salisbury steak

 Gouda

 Wednesday wine, beginner

2005
Cabernet Sauvignon
$15.99

Italy

ricossa

Life's a bit of a see-saw.
Your wine shouldn't be. We'll take the daily ups and downs, ride the peaks, and crest the valleys. But at the end of a long day all we ask is that we're afforded a glass of well-balanced wine. Just like the Ricossa B. d'A. Honest wine delivered for an honest price, oozing personality without demanding undue attention. Sip on! Sip on!

 steamed buns

 smoked salmon

 wine geek, winter warmer, rock out

2004
Barbera d'Asti
$16.00

blasted church

The oft second—nay, frequently third, commonly fourth—fiddle, Lemburger, gets a starring role in this straight-up, no frills, all-tasty BC blend from the house of wine worship, Blasted Church. A few buckets of Merlot mixed with the Burger softens the concoction of bright, brambly fruit flavours kissed with vanilla and lively with fresh acidity. "I made this wine for when Riedel breaks out its Big Gulp–sized 'O' Series," says winemaker Rich Kanazawa. A "Merburger" masterpiece if we ever tasted one. Dam Flood is damn fine.

 ribs

 aged cheddar

 rock out

2007
"The Dam Flood"
$16.99

France

château pesquié

Can a wine be a three wood and a nine iron at the same time? An habañero and a green pepper? A Madonna and a Justin Timberlake? Château Pesquié (*pes-kee-eh*, not *pes-kee*) masterfully mixes the best of two worlds, loading the bottle with a sensory odyssey from full throttle raspberry, ripe plum, and strawberry to a finesse of herbaceousness, orange peel, and sun-drenched fields. Head-on taste harmony.

 kebabs

 coq au vin

 winter warmer, BYO

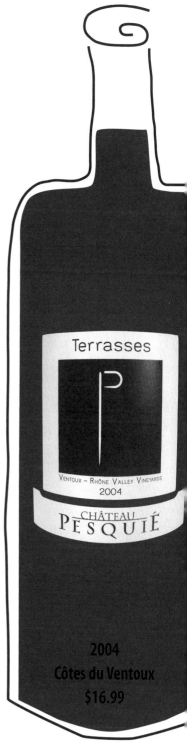

Terrasses

P

VENTOUX – RHÔNE VALLEY VINEYARDS
2004

CHÂTEAU
PESQUIÉ

2004
Côtes du Ventoux
$16.99

gabarda

Spain continues to be a dynamic source for great value bottles.

Up-and-coming regions abound across the country, and one of the latest areas we've been impressed with is Cariñena, the ruggedly handsome hinterland around Zaragoza. The Uno offers a total Garnacha (Grenache) hit—lots of raspberry, cherry, and lifted floral aromas followed by a Syrah punch of juicy and spicy flavours. Instant gratification wine, to be sure; it's pushing all the right sensory buttons.

 on its own

 duck confit

 BYO, beginner

2006
Cariñena
"Uno"
$16.99

Chile

novas

Let's hear it for compost teas and alternative pest management! The Novas 80/20 Carmenère and Cabernet Sauvignon blend is made from organically grown grapes in vineyards that brew their own organic compost and use a team of geese to go after unwanted insects. Funky and earthy on first whiff, the wine opens up to reveal rich plum flavours and a soft finish. We suggest three swigs for biodiversity.

 stew

 mushroom risotto

 romance

2004
Carmenère–Cabernet
Sauvignon
$16.99

pascual toso

You can only sample at the gelato counter so long before you start getting some annoyed looks from *nonno*. The way to taste it all (except for wasabi or curry, perhaps) is to pick up a bottle of Pascual Toso's Reserve Malbec. The astute "Had a Glasser" will remember Toso's regular Malbec a couple of issues ago, but newly available, massively delicious, and worth a few more bucks, this Malbec is a multi-flavoured mélange of chocolate, plum, coffee, vanilla, and a touch of toffee. An easy-drinking yet amply structured number. Put down the spoon and pick up a glass!

 roasted rack of lamb

 BYO, rock out

2006
Malbec
"Reserve"
$16.99

California

smoking loon

High-altitude sipping puts wine to the test.

Crammed in economy at ten thousand metres, ears popping, and palate on a serious sensory tailspin, aromas are dampened, flavours are dulled, and your bitter taste receptors are kicking. The usual vin de table is tough to swallow, and we wish they'd swap the little bottles for some Smoking Loon. The Syrah is all plush, soft fruit, and big aromas that will overcome any sinus issues. Most importantly though, this California cream is ultra easy to quaff anytime, whether you're at altitude or not.

 grilled eggplant with mint

 meatloaf

 romance, beginner

2006
Syrah
$17.00

sorrento

2006
Grenache
$17.00

Plug Sorrento into your wine touring GPS and you'll get one of three results: a mouthful of limpid Greco or Fiano from the rolling hillsides of Napoli, a mouthful of limpid Ortega or Optima from the shores of the Shuswap, or a drop kick to the maw from this McLaren Vale Grenache. The sheer amount of strawberry and muscle packed into this bottle is a slice of South Australian grape prowess—an endangered species in sub-$20 land, but tasted here in spades.

 braised chops

 on its own

 rock out, winter warmer

Australia

penfolds

Can a $100 wine be ten times better than a $10 wine? Emotional value aside, flavour for price is not linear. And this book is all about flavour for price, not about stocking your cellar with bottles that cobwebs appreciate more than you do. Let us explain. The paragon of Penfolds's portfolio, Grange, tastes great and goes well with lamb, but we can't vouch that it is 16 times better than this Shiraz-Cab. A mini-Grange, it's even made of the same grape varieties. Maybe the downgraded juice from Grange lands in Koonunga Hill? Maybe we're fantasizing. That this wine exudes delicious plum flavours with a peppery finish and is under $18 is no fantasy.

 roast

 winter warmer, rock out

2006
Shiraz-Cabernet
"Koonunga Hill"
$17.49

château peychaud

**2005
Bordeaux
$17.84**

Nobody makes a Bordeaux blend like the guys in Bordeaux. Around the globe, we hear "Bordeaux blend this" and "Bordeaux blend that" any time a winery puts Cabernet Sauvignon, Merlot, and Cabernet Franc (and sometimes Petit Verdot and Malbec) together in a bottle. Those are just varietal combinations that sound like Bordeaux—what's missing in the mix is geography. Bordeaux makes Bordeaux; everyone else makes Cab-Merlot. This bottle of Peychaud is Bordeaux through and through with its raspberry and pencil lead aromas, elegance, and full-on regality.

 grilled chicken

 Emmenthal

 beginner, romance

a-mano

Like the latest dance craze, Primitivo literally burst onto the wine scene. One day there was only Sangiovese; the next thing you knew, all the clubs were spinning the southern Italian grape skin. That was some years ago. Since then we've seen Primitivo appear and disappear, bottles strutting the shelves and then waning in popularity. Only a few survived. Krunk, Rio, and the like only lasted so long. A-Mano's Primitivo drops it like it's hot. The soft strawberry jam mixed with a dense, earthy goodness has life beyond synths and gangsta posturing. Crank that.

 tortellini with marinara

 pecorino

 BYO, winter warmer

2005
Primitivo
$17.99

boekenhout-skloof

The Porcupine Ridge is serious turbocharged value. Sure, there's some good souped-up sauce out there—some aromatic yeast or tannin powder because your Merlot is like a free-flow exhaust or a fancy cam in the Mazda. But nothing gets off the line like a well-balanced package of turbo, traction, and tires. Boeken's everyday-priced vinous gem rides low and focuses on custom craftsmanship to bring a noseful of rosemary, fennel, and cumin. Big, lush flavour, yet balanced in a super-drinkable package of tooth-staining goodness.

2006
Syrah
"Porcupine Ridge"
$17.99

 roast

 Morbier

 rock out, winter warmer

cusumano

Nero d'Avola is buddy wine. No, we're not trying to get cheeky with any family connections for this indigenous Sicilian grape. But Nero is typically brawny, yet in an approachable way—sun-baked earth and roast pepper folded into fruity and fleshy. Cusumano Nero d'Avola offers up the one-two bro greeting of a slap of savoury leather and pepper followed by a man hug of plush blackberry smoothness. Just don't call us "dude" when you pour us a glass.

 osso bucco

 patio/picnic, rock out

2006
Nero d'Avola
$17.99

galil mountain

2006
Cabernet Sauvignon
$17.99

If you're pining for modern Cabernet, we suggest you hit the Napa trail. If you want to taste postmodern Cabernet, Galil is your Deleuze, your Foucault, and your Devo. Though we can only read four words on the whole label, we're guessing that it's telling us that this is a no BS rendition of how CS should be made. As in: leave the jam and wood panelling for the pantry and concentrate on making just good Cab. We're talking cassis to the gills. There are gorgeous aromas of spice and herbs that speak to the merits of minimalism.

 rib roast

 grilled eggplant

 wine geek

viñaguareña

Good on this bottle for not succumbing to politically correct wine label linguistics. Too often these days proud, ethnocentric wine labels are getting poached, replaced by supposedly "consumer friendly" animals or geographic icons (pity the German wines in particular!). The two *ñ*'s in *Viñaguareña* mean all business, but they're really not hard to say (*veen-ya-gwa-rain-ya*). Plus, the old-school label perfectly captures the old-school sensibilities of this beast from Toro. A little stinky, and a lot of cigar, plum, and tar, this is a juicy and chewy wine with ample character.

 char sui

 goulash

 rock out, winter warmer

VIÑAGUAREÑA

Denominación de Origen TORO
Barrica 2003

2003
Toro
"Barrica"
$17.99

taurino

There's rustic wine—chock full of bramble, leather, earthy aromas—and then there's "refined rustic."

Nothing wrong with either. We'd happily sip a little liquid tillage and probably go for a second pour as long as a front-end loader came with the deal. But we reserve the term "refined rustic" for those special wines, the ones that have a little something besides just dirt. Taurino's splendid Salice is the pinnacle of this category, showing lots and lots and lots of earthy aromas, but some complementary slick licorice, dried fig, and strawberry smells as well. The package makes for some big flavour, but never without character.

**2003
Salice Salentino
$18.95**

 Brunswick stew

 wine geek, romance

Spain

montecillo

Taste this wine before it's extinct. The classic house of Montecillo still makes Rioja like they've got a DeLorean in the cellar and are waiting to go Back to the Future. Eschewing the current mountain of hype for plush, lush, fruit-packed, sweet vanilla-scented Rioja, Montecillo is like a liquid time machine back to those venerable dried cherry, old oak, even a bit raspy wines. Wines with character. The wines that we miss.

 rosemary chicken

 stew

 romance

**2003
Rioja
"Crianza"
$18.99**

paul jaboulet

If ever there was a tale of two Côtes du Rhônes, it's your wine tasting instructor telling you to queue this Jaboulet full of herbs and spices, plums, and cigars. Ethereal, transcendental, or whatever word you want to pull out of the thesaurus of wine adjectives. Then beside it, pour a glass of the Saint Cosme (reviewed on page 135) and get an entirely different mouthful of Rhône goodness. Voilà! A wine tasting of sorts. Swirl. Sip. It will make you look like you know what you're doing. It works for us.

 biryani

 Comté

 wine geek

2006
Côtes du Rhône
"Parallèle '45'"
$18.99

New Zealand

roy's hill

Time for a Merlot wake-up call. You know the ugly ducklings of the class, who are teased mercilessly as kids only to return to the reunion kicking ass? Shame on all you Merlot haters who jumped on the anti-Merlot bandwagon a few years back. Roy's Hill might no longer want to be your friend. Which would be your loss, because this is beautiful Merlot, tart and tangy with redcurrant and dried Chinese plum, rich and deep, complemented by a bright backbone that makes you stand up and take notice. Merlot all grown up and elegant. Time to get reacquainted with this noble grape!

 chops

 Monterey Jack

 BYO, patio/picnic

ROY'S HILL
HAWKES BAY
2006
MERLOT
CJ PASK WINERY

2006
Merlot
$18.99

tinhorn creek

***Solid* defines Tinhorn Creek.** Over the years, this southern Okanagan stop has continued to crank out tasty wines, from gut-warming reds to sweetly divine icewines. And the winery continues to push itself. Their latest Merlot is classic Tinhorn: big but nicely integrated oak, in your face red currant and raspberry fruit, and a muscle-ly tannic structure on the finish.

 chili con carne

 winter warmer, cellar

2005 Merlot $18.99

TINHORN CREEK
VINEYARDS

2005

MERLOT

ESTATE BOTTLED
RED WINE/VIN ROUGE
PRODUCT OF/PRODUIT DU : BRITISH COLUMBIA, CANADA

VQA OKANAGAN VALLEY VQA

cuatro pasos

If you're a grape geek, allow us to introduce Mencia. This red grape hails from Northwest Spain and has recently gained significant fame. Indeed, many a Mencia, typically in bottles from D.O. Bierzo, now command serious prices. Thankfully, you can check out the austere power and fresh fruit flavours common to Mencia by picking up a bottle of Cuatro Pasos. Savour its mix of caramel and earth, savoury leather and ripe fruit that have got the grape cognoscenti a-twitter.

 suckling pig

 machaca

 wine geek

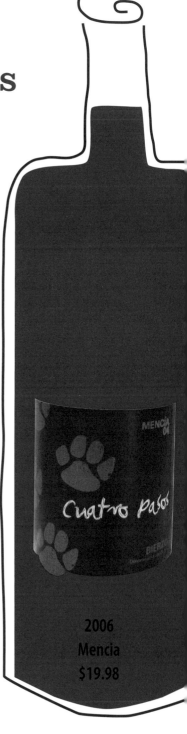

**2006
Mencia
$19.98**

carm

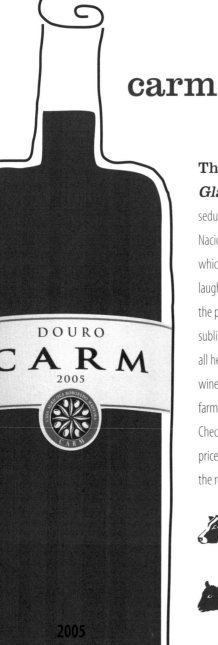

DOURO
CARM
2005

2005
Douro
$19.99

This is pure *Had a Glass* wine. Carm's Douro is a seductive blend of Portuguese Touriga Nacional, Tinta Roriz, and Touriga Franca which offers amazing value, almost laughably so. Many bottles going for twice the price get left in its lees. Super-complex, sublime structure, supple balance—it's all here. Not to mention this family-run wine and olive oil producer follows organic farming practices, so there's green cred too. Check it out before word spreads and the price inflates to make the bottle beyond the reach of our pages.

 BBQ tri-tip roast

 rack

 cellar, beginner

dehesa gago

Some years back we had the pleasure of rolling through Toro.

Parking the rental and strolling around the sun-blasted, quiet, and dusty streets of this small town in Spain's frontier land made us feel like we were playing out a scene from an old Paella Western. It also gave us an appreciation for the real sense of place Toro imbues in its massive, chunky reds. To get into the vibe, cue the Morricone and crack open a bottle of "G," a rich and suave bottle oozing black cherry and floral notes that elegantly captures the muscle of the region's strain of the Tempranillo grape.

2005
Toro
$19.99

 T-bone

 Manchego

 rock out, cellar, romance

South Africa

graham beck

We're not big on wine speak; no need to get hung up on special vocabulary to enjoy fermented grape juice.

But the "Old World" and "New World" distinctions do, we think, offer helpful stylistic guideposts. Google the terms if you like, or simply sip on this Shiraz, which deftly combines the creased leather, earth, and plum aromatics of the Old World with the juicy, smoky, pepper spice kick-in-the-pants drinkability of the New World. A real round the globe wine world tour in one glass.

 on its own

 roast

 beginner, winter warmer

2004
Shiraz
$19.99

Italy

masi

This is a wine curve-ball. Back in the days when we flogged wine in a shop, this is the bottle we steered regulars towards when they came in looking for "something different." The wine's character pulls the palate in lots of directions, with licorice and plum and a bright acidity to finish. Much of this uniqueness can be attributed to the special *ripasso* ("repassed" in Italian) winemaking style, lending the Campofiorin richness and character, and producing a wine slightly out of left field.

 falafel

 brescaola

 wine geek, BYO

2004
Veronese IGT
"Campofiorin"
$19.99

British Columbia

nk'mip cellars

If you think ordering off the wine list is intimidating, try saying "Nk'Mip" to the sommelier. This is when the point-at-item-on-menu-and-nod strategy works best. But despite any doubts about its pronunciation (say *in-ka-meep*), there is little doubt about the audaciousness of Nk'Mip's Merlot. BC steps up to the plate and hits a fruit-packed, food friendly bottle into the upper deck. Always an excellent choice.

 roast with garlic crust

 on its own

 romance, winter warmer

2005
Merlot
$19.99

saint cosme

Here's a wine critic's wine.

While we've never met Mr. Parker, we have read enough about the living legend of wine appraisal to figure that the guy likes his wines red and large-flavoured: the bigger the better. Ninety points for purple teeth; ninety-one if you get purple teeth *and* gums that feel like the Sahara. That's the image, anyway. We've got a theory that Mr. Parker goes home and sips Vinho Verde. Saint Cosme rocks the wine critics' palates because its fat, tarry flavour has the ability to resonate through any smokescreen of average wines. Its leathery grip puts a full nelson on your tongue, and yet you go back for more. Ninety-two points.

2006
Côtes du Rhône
$19.99

 steak sandwich

 on its own

 cellar

sandhill

2006 VINTAGE

SANDHILL

cabernet franc

SANDHILL ESTATE VINEYARD

VQA OKANAGAN VALLEY VQA

**2006
Cabernet Franc
$19.99**

If we ever get around to making a movie, the soundtrack will definitely include the Eagles' "Take It to the Limit." The track's got classic dude moment written all over it, and as we jam out in the karaoke room the wine in our glass will be Sandhill's voluptuous Cab Franc, which has seen 15 months' oak aging. That's enough to maim a lesser wine, but here it takes the plum, hint of leaf, graphite, and altogether fabulous expression of Cab Franc to the limit— with fine results.

 tartare

 mushroom steak

 rock out, wine geek

Austria

zantho

All 100 of these wines were tested on humans. Take this Zantho for instance, which we put through the "house party" test—an easy experiment that we highly recommend you try at home. Pop the corks on ten bottles, line them up on the counter, and throw a party. The first bottle that gets emptied makes the Top 100 cut, and the rest we use to braise the main course. Zantho's earthy, herby, tart-berry Zweigelt outperformed its competition by a surprising margin, beating the second place Cabernet by a solid 330 millilitres.

 braised chicken

 chops

 wine geek

2001
Zweigelt
$19.99

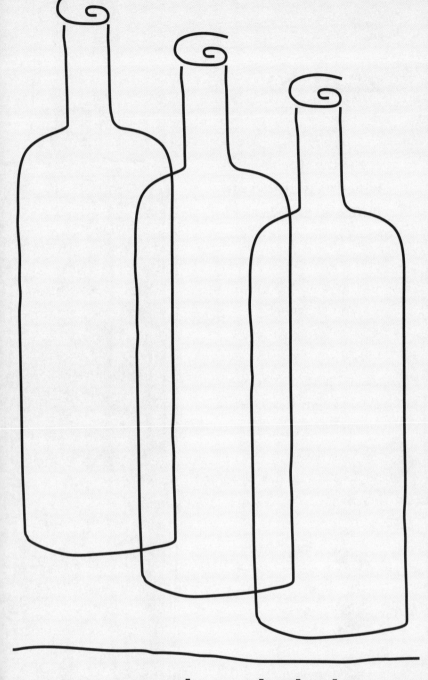

the bubblies

hungaria

Like Monaco's Grand Prix, celebrating with a shower of champagne (Moët, if we're not mistaken), the Hungarian F1 uses, well, Hungaria. It tastes just as good, and you can soak five times as many people for the same price. Did we mention that the winner of the last race was driving a Yaris? It's the synergy of class and common sense that we love about the Hungaria. And it sure beats milk at the Indy.

 on its own

 pepperoni pizza

 BYO, Wednesday wine

**Brut
"Grande Cuvée"
$13.90**

Australia

jacob's creek

The last time we were in Oz, two memorable things happened. One was listening to a scratchy Neil Young's *Harvest* on an old record player in a winery guesthouse while drinking bottle after bottle of Eden Valley Riesling. The second was getting a glass of bubble shoved into our fists every time we turned around. Australians are crazy for bubble—and the occasional Canadian classic rocker. The folks at Jacob's Creek stop at nothing to foster a sophisticated bubble curriculum, right down to a traditional in-bottle second ferment—an effort not always seen in a $17 job. The result is a bubble that's big on fruit, with plenty of punch and a soft finish.

Chardonnay–Pinot Noir
"Brut Cuvée"
$16.99

 on its own

 romance, patio/picnic

beato bartolomeo

If we could get one wine on tap all the time, it'd be Prosecco.
What could be better than to slide up to any bar, any time of the day, for a frothy pint of Pro? It would go perfectly with the bar nuts. If there happened to be a little Parmigiano Reggiano and Iberico ham instead, we wouldn't complain. Then, if the bartender pulled the Beato tap, well that would have us happier than pigs in mud.

 on its own

 figs with goat cheese

 patio/picnic, aperitif

Prosecco
$19.99

the black chook

Rejoice, there's another sparkling Shiraz on our shelves. Rejoice, rejoice, it's delightfully tasty! That's like Christmas in July—which is what it's sort of like in Australia—where sparkling Shiraz is typically served with the turkey. That's one great occasion, and we can think of three more right off (party, cheese plate, Wednesday) when we'd happily imbibe the Chook's full-bodied, berrylicious, caramel-on-the-finish flavour assault.

 turkey dinner, duck

 nachos

 rock out, Wednesday wine

Sparkling Shiraz
$19.99

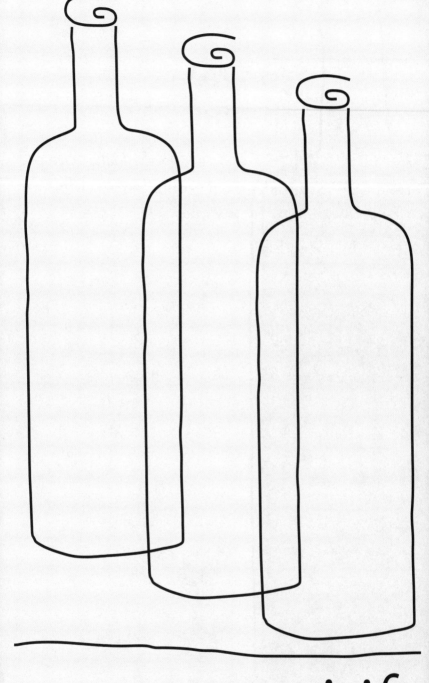

the aperitifs

gonzález byass

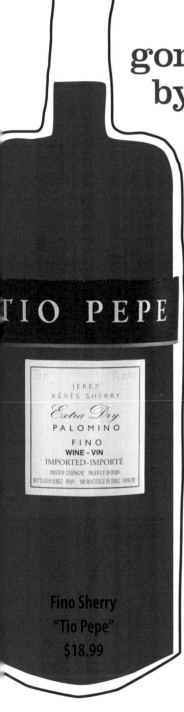

JEREZ
XÉRÉS SHERRY
Extra Dry
PALOMINO
FINO
WINE - VIN
IMPORTED-IMPORTÉ
PRODUIT D'ESPAGNE   PRODUCT OF SPAIN
BOTTLED IN JEREZ · SPAIN   MIS BOUTEILLE EN JEREZ · ESPAGNE

Fino Sherry
"Tio Pepe"
$18.99

If we were a *lucha libre* wrestling tag team, our *nom de guerre* would be "The Tio Pepes." Then the Uncle Pepes would school the kids, flying clotheslines from the top ropes. Still, to show we were civilized wrestlers, our training routine would include a daily 4 p.m. sherry break. We'd break out the bottle of Tio Pepe from the fridge, pour a *copita*, and sip as we reviewed our fight films to strengthen our moves. We'd slap our tights and smack our lips, enjoying the bracingly dry and tangy, nutty allure of this classic fino sherry (though it might prove hard to drink through our masks).

 on its own

 toasted walnuts

 patio/picnic, wine geek, beginner

France

lillet

"Servir très frais." We like a bottle that comes with operating instructions. The world seems to be warming to aperitifs, a trend we'll happily partake in. With the resurgence of serious cocktail culture, barkeeps are even starting to create their own special blends. Indeed, much thought and work goes into refining each aperitif's secret recipe, but until you decide to work out your own, we suggest starting your evening with Lillet, a blend of wine and fruit liqueurs. Follow the bottle: pour directly from the fridge, over rocks if you like, and feel free to garnish with an orange twist.

 on its own

 romance, rock out

Apéritif
$19.99

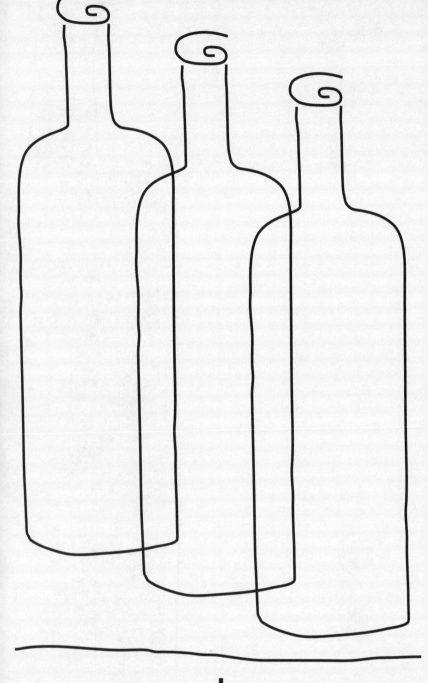

the desserts

France

st. rémy

Pity the brandy. How many people even own snifters? True, there was a mid-90s niche fascination with Cognac and other high-end brandies stemming from hip-hop shout outs, but we fear brandy has gone the way of backwards-worn pants. Time for a brandy revival! Start easy. Pick up a bottle of amber-coloured, caramel- and candied orange–flavoured Napoleon, which is blended and distilled from a myriad of grapes before being aged in oak. Perfect for the trifle, to spike the punch, or to sip as a nightcap.

 mud pie

 shrimp cocktail

 romance, patio/picnic

**V.S.O.P. Brandy
"Napoleon"
$11.00
(375 mL)**

tyrrell's wines

Tawny is a multi-tasker.

We like keeping a bottle of Tawny Port around because it's so versatile and delicious. You can pour a lug of Tawny at the end of the night and kick back with a little Jim Noir vibing off the vacuum tube amp. You can also incorporate it right into a meal, using a little splash as the secret ingredient in sauces to kick up the complexity. Like sherry, it works particularly well with anything involving mushrooms or melted cheese. You may as well pour a splash into the chef's cup at the same time. The rich kumquat and raisiny goodness of this great-value Tawny makes it an enjoyable all-rounder.

Tawny Port
"Special Aged"
$15.49

 crème brûlée

 brie, Gorgonzola

 BYO, winter warmer

graham's

A full-fledged sensory sledgehammer, the Graham's Six Grapes comes at you like a flavour freight train, but one that leaves your palate all warm and fuzzy. Taken from the vintage Port lots but tailored to be drunk now, the Six Grapes concept Port fuses bigness and smoothness (our two favourite wine tasting terms) to appease those who can't wait for their vintage to ripen and want more love than those LBVs.

 plain dark chocolate

 blue cheese

 romance, winter warmer

**Port
"Six Grapes"
$16.99
(375 mL)**

château la rame

Bring on the ass pocket of sticky. What's better than a hip flask of whisky, you ask? Why, a half-bottle of unctuous, elegant sweet Bordeaux. We're telling you, whip this bottle out as an interlude to any romantic, moonlit walk, and you're so money. Of course, you'll have to remember to bring a corkscrew, but once you're into the bottle there's no stopping the luxurious lifted floral and golden sultana aromas. Your tongue will get tied by this super-honeyed, anise-filled beauty. But a word of caution: it might not fit in the back of skinny jeans.

2003
Sainte Croix du Mont
$17.99
(375mL)

 on its own

 fondue

 romance, rock out

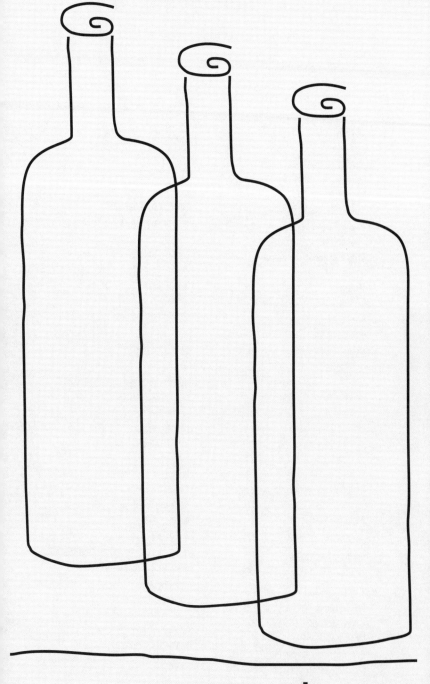

the indices

wines by country

Argentina

Don Miguel Gascón Syrah 107
Finca los Primos Chardonnay 47
Pascual Toso Malbec "Reserve" 114
Trapiche Sauvignon Blanc–Semillon "Astica" 46
Trivento Malbec-Syrah-Bonarda "Amado Sur" 103

Australia

Banrock Station Shiraz-Mataro 85
Black Chook Sparkling Shiraz 142
d'Arenberg "Stump Jump White" 56
Jacob's Creek Chardonnay–Pinot Noir "Brut Cuvée" 140
Lindemans Shiraz "Reserve" 105
Long Flat White Semillon–Sauvignon Blanc 49
Penfolds Shiraz-Cabernet "Koonunga Hill" 117
Sorrento Grenache 116
Thirsty Lizard Shiraz 97
Tyrrell's Wines Tawny Port "Special Aged" 148
Wolf Blass Riesling 58

Austria

Hiedler Grüner Veltliner 75
Zantho Zweigelt 137

British Columbia

Blasted Church "The Dam Flood" 110
Golden Mile Cellars Chardonnay 74
Nk'mip Cellars Merlot 134
Quails' Gate Chardonnay 70
Red Rooster Pinot Blanc 61
Sandhill Cabernet Franc 136
See Ya Later Ranch Gewürztraminer 62

St. Hubertus Chasselas 60
Summerhill Pinot Gris 72
Tinhorn Creek Merlot 128

California

Barefoot Pinot Grigio 48
Cline Viognier 65
Smoking Loon Syrah 115

Chile

Anakena Carmenère 93
Concha y Toro Chardonnay "Casillero del Diablo" 51
Cono Sur Chardonnay 55
Cousiño Macul Sauvignon Gris 66
Morandé Cabernet Sauvignon–Syrah Rosé "Pionero" 80
Novas Carmenère–Cabernet Sauvignon 113
Terra Andina Cabernet-Merlot 86

France

Brumont Gros Manseng-Sauvignon 59
Chanson Mâcon Villages 73
Château Haut Perthus Bergerac 95
Château la Gravette Rosé Minervois 81
Château La Rame Sainte Croix du Mont 150
Château Pesquié Côtes du Ventoux 111
Château Peychaud Bordeaux 118
Chat-en-Oeuf Côtes du Ventoux 96
Lillet Apéritif 145
Louis Bernard Côtes du Rhône 102
Louis Latour Chardonnay "Ardèche" 52
Paul Jaboulet "Parallèle '45'" Côtes du Rhône 126
Paul Mas Viognier 53
Pierre Sparr Gewürztraminer 76
Saint Cosme Côtes du Rhône 135
St. Rémy V.S.O.P. Brandy "Napoleon" 147

Germany

St. Urbans-Hof Riesling 78
St. Ursula Dornfelder–Pinot Noir "Goldener Oktober" 88

Valckenberg Gewürztraminer 64

Greece
Boutari Moschofilero 69

Hungary
Hungaria Brut "Grande Cuvée" 139

Israel
Galil Mountain Cabernet Sauvignon 122

Italy
A-Mano Primitivo 119
Beato Bartolomeo Prosecco 141
Caldora Montepulciano d'Abruzzo 91
Casal Thaulero Montepulciano d'Abruzzo 87
Cusumano Nero d'Avola 121
Di Lenardo Pinot Grigio 67
Donnafugata Sicilia "Anthilia" 68
Flaio Primitivo 92
Folonari Valpolicella 98
Masi Veronese IGT "Campofiorin" 133
Montalto Nero d'Avola–Cabernet Sauvignon 90
Ricossa Barbera d'Asti 109
Taurino Salice Salentino 124
Tormaresca Chardonnay 57

New Zealand
Oyster Bay Merlot Rosé 82
Roy's Hill Merlot 127
Shepherds Ridge Sauvignon Blanc 77

Portugal
Azul Bairrada 106
Carm Douro 130
Graham's Port "Six Grapes" 149
José Maria da Fonseca Periquita 89

South Africa
Beyerskloof Pinotage 99
Boekenhoutskloof Syrah "Porcupine Ridge" 120
Excelsior Cabernet Sauvignon 108
Golden Kaan Shiraz 94

Graham Beck Shiraz 132
KWV Roodeberg 101
Saxenburg "Guinea Fowl" 71
Teddy Hall Chenin Blanc 63
Winery of Good Hope Chenin Blanc 54

Spain
Cuatro Pasos Mencia 129
Dehesa Gago Toro 131
Espelt Garnacha-Cariñena "Sauló" 100
Gabarda Cariñena "Uno" 112
González Byass Fino Sherry "Tio Pepe" 144
Luzón Jumilla 104
Montecillo Rioja "Crianza" 125
Segura Viudas Rosado Brut "Lavit" 83
Viñaguareña Toro "Barrica" 123
Viñedos Raimat Albariño-Chardonnay 50

wines by type

Albariño-Chardonnay
Viñedos Raimat 50

Bairrada
Azul 106

Barbera d'Asti
Ricossa 109

Bordeaux
Château Peychaud 118

Brandy
St. Rémy "Napoleon" 147

Cabernet Franc
Sandhill 136

Cabernet-Merlot
Terra Andina 86

Cabernet Sauvignon
Excelsior 108
Galil Mountain 122

Cariñena
Gabarda "Uno" 112

Carm Douro 130
Château Haut Perthus Bergerac 95
José Maria da Fonseca Periquita 89
KWV Roodeberg 101
Luzón Jumilla 104
Masi Veronese IGT "Campofiorin" 133
St. Ursula Dornfelder—Pinot Noir
  "Goldener Oktober" 88
Trivento Malbec-Syrah-Bonarda "Amado
  Sur" 103

Riesling
St. Urbans-Hof Mosel Saar Ruwer 78
Wolf Blass 58

Rioja
Montecillo "Crianza" 125

Rosé
Château la Gravette Minervois 81
Morandé Cabernet Sauvignon—Syrah
  Rosé "Pionero" 80
Oyster Bay Merlot Rosé 82
Segura Viudas Rosado Brut "Lavit" 83

Sauvignon Blanc
Shepherds Ridge 77

Sauvignon Gris
Cousiño Macul 66

Sherry
González Byass "Tio Pepe" 144

Shiraz
Golden Kaan 94
Graham Beck 132
Lindemans "Reserve" 105
Thirsty Lizard 97

Shiraz-Cabernet
Penfolds "Koonunga Hill" 117

Sparkling
Hungaria Brut "Grande Cuvée" 139
Beato Bartolomeo Prosecco 141
Black Chook Sparkling Shiraz 142

Jacob's Creek Chardonnay—Pinot Noir
  "Brut Cuvée" 140
Segura Viudas Rosado Brut "Lavit" 83

Syrah
Boekenhoutskloof "Porcupine Ridge" 120
Don Miguel Gascón 107
Smoking Loon 115

Tempranillo
Dehesa Gago Toro 131
Viñaguareña Toro "Barrica" 123

Valpolicella
Folonari 98

Viognier
Cline 65
Paul Mas 53

White Blend
Brumont Gros Manseng-Sauvignon 59
d'Arenberg "Stump Jump White" 56
Donnafugata Sicilia "Anthìlia" 68
Long Flat White Semillon—Sauvignon
  Blanc 49
Saxenburg "Guinea Fowl" 71
Trapiche Sauvignon Blanc—Semillon
  "Astica" 46

Zweigelt
Zantho 137

wines by food

Beef
A-Mano Primitivo 119
Anakena Carmenère 93
Beyerskloof Pinotage 99
Boekenhoutskloof Syrah "Porcupine
  Ridge" 120
Carm Douro 130
Casal Thaulero Montepulciano d'Abruzzo
  87
Château Haut Perthus Bergerac 95

Château la Gravette Rosé Minervois 81
Château Pesquié Côtes du Ventoux 111
Cuatro Pasos Mencia 129
Cusumano Nero d'Avola 121
Dehesa Gago Toro 131
Don Miguel Gascón Syrah 107
Espelt Garnacha-Cariñena "Sauló" 100
Excelsior Cabernet Sauvignon 108
Flaio Primitivo 92
Galil Mountain Cabernet Sauvignon 122
Graham Beck Shiraz 132
José Maria da Fonseca Periquita 89
KWV Roodeberg 101
Long Flat White Semillon–Sauvignon
    Blanc 49
Luzón Jumilla 104
Masi Veronese IGT "Campofiorin" 133
Montecillo Rioja "Crianza" 125
Nk'mip Cellars Merlot 134
Novas Carmenère–Cabernet Sauvignon
    113
Oyster Bay Merlot Rosé 82
Saint Cosme Côtes du Rhône 135
Sandhill Cabernet Franc 136
Smoking Loon Syrah 115
St. Ursula Dornfelder–Pinot Noir
    "Goldener Oktober" 88
Tinhorn Creek Merlot 128
Trivento Malbec-Syrah-Bonarda "Amado
    Sur" 103
Viñaguareña Toro "Barrica" 123

Cheese

A-Mano Primitivo 119
Beato Bartolomeo Prosecco 141
Black Chook Sparkling Shiraz 142
Blasted Church "The Dam Flood" 110
Boekenhoutskloof Syrah "Porcupine
    Ridge" 120
Château Haut Perthus Bergerac 95
Château Peychaud Bordeaux 118
Dehesa Gago Toro 131

Excelsior Cabernet Sauvignon 108
Graham's Port "Six Grapes" 149
KWV Roodeberg 101
Lindemans Shiraz "Reserve" 105
Louis Bernard Côtes du Rhône 102
Paul Jaboulet "Parallèle '45'" Côtes du
    Rhône 126
Red Rooster Pinot Blanc 61
Roy's Hill Merlot 127
See Ya Later Ranch Gewürztraminer 62
St. Ursula Dornfelder–Pinot Noir
    "Goldener Oktober" 88
Teddy Hall Chenin Blanc 63
Thirsty Lizard Shiraz 97
Tyrrell's Wines Tawny Port "Special Aged"
    148

Chocolate

Château La Rame Sainte Croix du Mont
    150
Graham's Port "Six Grapes" 149
St. Rémy V.S.O.P. Brandy "Napoleon" 147
Tyrrell's Wines Tawny Port "Special Aged"
    148

Fish

Boutari Moschofilero 69
Brumont Gros Manseng-Sauvignon 59
Château la Gravette Rosé Minervois 81
Louis Latour Chardonnay "Ardèche" 52
Ricossa Barbera d'Asti 109
Summerhill Pinot Gris 72
Winery of Good Hope Chenin Blanc 54

Lamb

Carm Douro 130
Golden Kaan Shiraz 94
Pascual Toso Malbec "Reserve" 114
Paul Jaboulet "Parallèle '45'" Côtes du
    Rhône 126
Penfolds Shiraz-Cabernet "Koonunga
    Hill" 117
Roy's Hill Merlot 127
Sorrento Grenache 116

Di Lenardo Pinot Grigio 67
Donnafugata Sicilia "Anthilia" 68
Louis Latour Chardonnay "Ardèche" 52
Morandé Cabernet Sauvignon–Syrah
    Rosé "Pionero" 80
St. Hubertus Chasselas 60
St. Rémy V.S.O.P. Brandy "Napoleon" 147
St. Urbans-Hof Riesling 78
Teddy Hall Chenin Blanc 63
Trapiche Sauvignon Blanc–Semillon
    "Astica" 46
Viñedos Raimat Albariño-Chardonnay 50

Sandhill Cabernet Franc 136
Smoking Loon Syrah 115
Tormaresca Chardonnay 57

Spicy

Boutari Moschofilero 69
Chat-en-Oeuf Côtes du Ventoux 96
Cono Sur Chardonnay 55
Cousiño Macul Sauvignon Gris 66
d'Arenberg "Stump Jump White" 56
Hungaria Brut "Grande Cuvée" 139
Lindemans Shiraz "Reserve" 105
St. Urbans-Hof Riesling 78
Valckenberg Gewürztraminer 64

Vegetarian

Banrock Station Shiraz-Mataro 85
Barefoot Pinot Grigio 48
Beyerskloof Pinotage 99
Caldora Montepulciano d'Abruzzo 91
Flaio Primitivo 92
Folonari Valpolicella 98
Galil Mountain Cabernet Sauvignon 122
González Byass Fino Sherry "Tio Pepe" 144
Long Flat White Semillon–Sauvignon
    Blanc 49
Masi Veronese IGT "Campofiorin" 133
Montalto Nero d'Avola–Cabernet
    Sauvignon 90
Novas Carmenère–Cabernet Sauvignon
    113
Paul Mas Viognier 53
Pierre Sparr Gewürztraminer 76
Quails' Gate Chardonnay 70

acknowledgements

This fourth edition of *Had a Glass* would never have gotten a swirl if the authors were serving it up alone. And though it may sound like we've hit "repeat" on many of our thank yous, the repetition is testament to the relationships we've forged with a great group of people that help inspire and make this book happen.

Once again we'd like to extend our gratitude to Robert and the hard-working staff at Whitecap. A high-five to Melva who meticulously edited the book, ensuring we never rambled aimlessly. A toast to Michelle, Taryn, and Grace for keeping us on schedule (even if that meant extending a deadline here or there). And a shout-out to Jan, who kept the endless number of wine labels on track and Photoshopped her way through them, and again to Jacqui, who dropped some great design on these pages. Finally, because bottles of wine are not light, and there are cases upon cases of wines to be tasted for a book like *Had a Glass*, we would like to extend an arm curl of thanks to Brian and Meghan for their heavy lifting above and beyond the call of duty.

This year's recipes were generously provided by some of our favourite cooks, and we are indebted to them and their culinary know-how. Family and friends continue to provide invaluable support by relating their wine experiences, giving us feedback on our reviews, and (enthusiastically) volunteering their tasting expertise. And Mai and Karen provide an amazing foundation of encouragement, urging our palates to continue exploring.

We'd like to extend thanks to the agents, wineries, and marketing boards that have supported us in this venture. We hope new and exciting wines will continue to land on our shores and spring from your cellars—this is what makes wine drinking worthwhile. Also, a clink of the glass to the local wine media, who acknowledge our cause and have supported us wholeheartedly since our days of toque-wearing wine drinking. We have had the pleasure of publishing in a number of venues, and special thanks goes to *The Province* for giving the "Wine Guys" a weekly home, as well as the BC Liquor Control Board's *TASTE* Magazine.

Lastly, we salute the wine shops, tasting rooms, bookstores, and others who keep the wine love flowing.